# FEASTING NATURALLY

## WITH OUR FRIENDS

**by**

*Mary Ann Pickard*

**illustrated by**

*Marsha Holcomb*

distributed by
**Southern Star, Inc.**
P.O. Box 968
Harrison, Arkansas 72601

First Printing August 1982 - 5,000

Copyright © 1982 by Mary Ann Pickard

Printed by
Cookbook Publishers, Inc.
Lenexa, Kansas

Library of Congress Catalog Number 82-060390
ISBN Number 0-934474-24-9

Humble yourselves, therefore, under the mighty hand of God, that He may exalt you at the proper time, casting all your anxieties upon Him because He cares for you.

I Peter 5:6-7 ASV

TABLE OF CONTENTS

You are invited
to enjoy
the pleasure of
Feasting Naturally
with our friends

Can it be that this is the third *Feasting Naturally* book in as many years? When Bill and I took a step of faith and published the first book, we never dreamed the demand would be so great! Without a doubt, the greatest blessing to us has been the response from our readers.

For that reason, preparing this book for you has been an absolute delight! Everything in it, save a few hints and footnotes, has come from *Feasting Naturally* readers, and that fact alone makes this a truly unique publication. In addition, each recipe has been carefully tested by me or one of my team of topnotch cooks who helped me test recipes. Some were tested two or even three times, just to be sure. If the results were not a resounding "yes" or as one friend described hers, "yummy, yummy yes", they were not included in this collection.

And what a collection this is! The ideas and combinations are as diversified as the places from which they came! You might notice that there are no recipes from me in this book. I was tempted to put in a few really unique recipes I've created lately, but decided against it. I'm saving my ideas for my newsletter, which will be published in January '83 (see **Special Offers** for details). Besides, my readers came up with such a fantastic variety of recipes, I was glad to have an opportunity to function as editor! Of course, you can be confident that the ingredients will include no refined sugars, flours or food grains, and few if any harmful flavorings, colorings, additives or preservatives[1].

Allow me to remind you, briefly, why the foods listed above are not included in a carefully chosen diet. Refined sugar, to begin with, has no nutritional value but lots of calories. Because of the calories, it will give you quick energy, but that energy is short-lived. When a concentrated carbohydrate such as a candy bar is digested, the blood sugar level rises significantly (this is the quick energy phase) but is swiftly corrected by the mediating effect of insulin secretion. The problem is that insulin overreacts to the surge of sugar and overcorrects, driving the blood sugar level down and producing low blood sugar[2].

---

[1]Occasionally a recipe will call for canned soups or Worcestershire sauce— read labels of canned soups carefully and use sparingly, Worcestershire sauce is listed as optional. It does contain some sugar, so you may want to use chili powder or cayenne pepper with a little honey instead. Tamari soy sauce will also substitute for it.

[2]Low blood sugar, also called hypoglycemia, can be a temporary or reactionary condition which corrects either in time, by eating foods high in protein which will be released into the blood-stream as sugars more slowly, or by eating more sugar. The trouble with the last solution is that it produces the whole cycle again. And it is, therefore, not an acceptable solution.

Hypoglycemia can also be a clinical problem which can be identified by a 6-hour glucose tolerance test and treated with dietary restrictions.

PREFACE

Producing symptoms which range from depression to allergies[3], this condition can masquerade as a dozen different physical or emotional disorders, when often a simple change in diet can affect a significant difference in overall health.

Most seriously, hypoglycemia or low blood sugar is a precursor to diabetes, which is currently running rampant in our refined western culture. On top of that fact, add the classic argument that sugar consumption precipitates dental disease[4]. It also depletes B vitamin stores, is addictive, contributes to obesity, and replaces valuable foods in the diet. More evidence is uncovered each year linking excessive sugar consumption to heart disease, cancer, hyperactivity, schizophrenia, alcoholism, and learning disorders. Let's face it, the only good thing you can say about sugar is that it tastes good, and even that argument doesn't stand after one has rid his body of sugars and lost the taste for them.

Refined flours and food grains should be avoided because they are nutritionally deficient. The refining process mills out the bran and germ, which are loaded with nutrients and essential for proper digestion. A token of nutrients enrich the product[5], but the whole process is ineffective at best. In addition, refined flours and grains are basic carbohydrates, easily converted to glucose. For someone who is sensitive to sugar, they can create the same conditions and results as sugar.

Simply eliminating these products completely from your diet will have a positive effect on you, probably within three weeks. Add a carefully chosen aerobic exercise program and some sunshine, and you will be a new person— in touch with your body again. I know this to be true because I have experienced it myself. My particular experience is not especially dramatic, it just includes a quiet satisfaction that I am treating my body in the best manner possible, which is enough for me.

However, our family has experienced a dramatic change which opened our eyes to the ideas I am sharing with you. Just a few short years ago Bill, my husband, was caught in a thunderous whirlwind of obesity, physical inactivity, and intense stress. His physical and emotional equilibrium was threatened by one blood sugar crisis after another[6], eventually leading to severe chest pains. When the gravity of his condition touched me, I asked the Lord for help. He responded to my prayer by giving Bill the power to overcome his addiction to

---

[3]Symptoms can include depression, anxiety, narcolepsy, insomnia, lack of sexual drive, fast or noticeable heartbeat, itching or crawling sensations, cold sweats, tremors, muscle pains, inability to concentrate, forgetfulness, numbness, fainting or blackouts, convulsions and allergies.

[4]The most harm done by sugary foods occurs in the first 20 minutes after they are eaten, when plaque in the mouth combines with the sugar to create acid. Therefore, rinsing the mouth thoroughly and/or cleaning teeth and gums after **any** sweet or sticky food is a good habit to develop.

[5]Niacin, thiamine, riboflavin and iron are added back, but the germ contains a wealth of B vitamins, protein, vitamin E and lecithin.

[6]We later found him to have functional or reactive hypoglycemia, a condition which produces low blood sugar symptoms when refined sugars and grains are eaten.

sugar and set his life on an even keel with a carefully chosen diet[7]. In the process he lost fifty pounds and gained a whole new feeling about life itself. We began to realize how brutally we had treated our bodies by abusing them with deficient foods and little exercise. The Lord continued to gently guide our thoughts until He impressed me to share them in a book and, well, you know the rest. *Feasting Naturally* and all that it has meant to our family belongs to Him, and that is why it is so precious to me.

You are probably saying to yourself, "That's fine for her family, but I'm too busy to do all that cooking, my husband would never eat all that stuff; and my children are too old to change. I could never do that". Well, let me tell you that you certainly **can!** It may be necessary for you to go "cold turkey" as we did, and throw all the junk foods out. If you have serious problems such as Bill had, it will certainly be necessary. But I rarely recommend that approach, especially when children are already school age. Unless the problems are so severe that everyone is willing to try anything, a "cold turkey" approach will only cause rebellion.

Start gradually; take a step at a time. Use your local grocery or specialty store to help you. Plan your time and menus to include old favorites as well as new tastes. Don't demand clean plates; just pleasantly offer a bite of a new dish and see that it is at least tasted.

I am listing three levels of change and a possible progression for you to follow in modifying your family's eating habits. You may feel comfortable with Level II and never go on to Level III; at least you will be aware of what your family is getting and in control of your nutrition. Level III is not difficult to achieve. I do not spend all my time in the kitchen; with four children, three books and all the extra activities, I don't have the time. Use the ideas in *Feasting Naturally* books, and you won't need to spend all your time in the kitchen either.

**Level I**

| Instead of . . . . . . . . . . . . . . . . . . . . . | Try |
| --- | --- |
| candy bars | fresh fruit |
| | peanuts |
| sugary cereals | Grape-Nuts™ |
| | Nutri-grain™ |
| | Shredded wheat |
| | Granola |
| Cola drinks | Shasta™ drinks made with fructose |
| | corn syrup |

---

[7]We have chosen to follow the "Optimal Diet" as defined by Cheraskin and Ringsdorf in *Psychodietetics*. It recommends complex carbohydrates, proteins and fats which break down in the body more slowly than sugar to be the best choices: meats, cheeses, dairy products, nuts, and seeds, vegetables and fruits, legumes, cereals, and whole grains. Sweeteners such as honey and fructose are recommended when necessary; caffeine laden beverages and salt are to be used a minimum amount.

**Level I** *(Continued)*

Instead of . . . . . . . . . . . . . . . . . . . . . Try

frozen sugared pops              frozen fruit juice in pop containers

hamburgers & French fries        salad bars

white bread                      whole wheat, pumpernickel or rye
                                 (heavy breads)

sugar in tea, etc.               honey

**Level II**

chocolate                        carob[8]

white rice                       brown or wild rice

packaged breads[9]               homemade muffins (quick and easy, full
                                 of whole grain goodness)

canned vegetables                fresh steamed or stir fried vegetables

ice cream or pudding             yogurt

sweetened desserts               fresh fruit and cheese; honey
(occasionally okay,              sweetened ice creams and puddings
birthdays, etc.)

cola drinks                      sodas made with juice concentrate
                                 and Club soda (1¼ c. concentrate to 1
                                 qt. soda)

**Level III**

sugar, brown sugar,              honey, 100% maple syrup, fructose,
molasses, corn syrup,            juice concentrates, date sugar,
dextrins, dextrose               raisin syrup[10]

enriched pasta                   whole grain pasta

lots of red meat                 chicken, fish, combination of
                                 proteins

bought bread                     homemade bread

---

[8]Carob is sweeter than chocolate, very high in calcium, nonallergenic, has very little fat content and no caffeine. It also costs the same as cocoa and can be used in the same ways.

[9]It is possible to find packaged 100% whole wheat breads without sugar. It is easier and more economical to make your own.

[10]Sugars listed on the left contain a high proportion of sucrose which will elevate the blood sugar level. Sugars on the right will not do that unless taken in excess, with the exception of fructose which will not elevate it at all. Remember that the best sweetener is none at all, so use even the acceptable ones with discretion. Avoid saccharins; use sorbitol if necessary only on occasion (sugar free gum, etc.).

**Level III** *(Continued)*

Instead of .....................Try

caffeine laden coffee & tea            herb tea, fruit slushes, water

lettuce all the time                   sprouts

convenience foods                      home prepared foods

I challenge you to commit yourself to changing your diet now—either gradually or drastically. And do something nice for your body for a change. Don't demand your children to do something you haven't demanded of yourself. As parents, we need to be concerned about our children's nutritional education, just as we care about their emotional, physical, spiritual, educational and artistic training. Remember "we are what we eat". Imagine how you feel after consuming a hamburger[11], French fries and a big chocolate shake. Now imagine you have just finished a fresh fruit plate with whole grain muffins and cheese wedges. The choice is yours.

---

[11]Of course it is possible to have a delicious and healthy hamburger on a whole grain bun without the sugary condiments usually added.

**Editor's Note:** For consistency, I have notated "oil" rather than a particular kind of oil except when it needs to be olive oil for taste. My personal preference is safflower oil, and I recommend it to you because it contains all the essential fatty acids.

Some contributors specified sea salt or noninstant dry milk; I edited it salt and powdered milk, leaving the choice to you.

---

As with any dietary suggestions, consult your physician before beginning anything this book advocates, especially if you are a diabetic requiring insulin.

My sincere appreciation goes to you, my readers, who contributed the tempting recipes which compose this superb collection. Sharing a little part of you with me has made you very special to me, and I hope you delight in the results as much as I do.

I was able to function as an editor for this book solely because of the outstanding team of topnotch cooks and friends who helped me test over 600 recipes. I am deeply grateful for the cheerful contribution of Jan, Becky, Jane, Sue, Coleen, Cheryl, Karen, and Lou.

Without the versatile staff at Bill's office, the manuscript would not have been properly prepared. Special thanks for that go to Linda, Barbi, Carolyn, Nancy, and Donita.

My proofreaders, Joe, Lou, and Karen, managed to find all kinds of unclarified thoughts and misspelled words. You have them to thank, as I do, for the accuracy of this manuscript.

Special thanks to Marsha Holcomb, who stepped into an emergency situation, took over the project of illustrating the book and completed it beautifully in record time. I'm so grateful to have been able to depend on her consistently.

But most important of all is my family who totally loves and supports me in what is truly a family endeavor. Jennifer, Jeremy, Jamie, and our newly adopted foster son Walt have managed to keep understanding and loving me through all the deadlines; I couldn't ask for more loving children. And thank you, Bill, for being you— for being so proud and supportive, and for lifting me up before I even stumble. I love you all so much.

ACKNOWLEDGMENTS

BREADS

# APPLE WHOLE WHEAT WAFFLES

2 c. whole wheat flour
1/2 tsp. salt
1 Tbsp. baking powder
1/2 tsp. cinnamon
1/2 tsp. nutmeg
1/4 tsp. cloves

1 Tbsp. honey
2/3 c. powdered milk
2 eggs
1/3 c. oil
1 tsp. vanilla
1 medium apple, cored and chopped
1 3/4 c. apple juice

Combine first 6 ingredients. Pulverize apple and remaining ingredients in blender. Combine liquid and dry ingredients, mixing well. Bake in waffle iron.

Preparation time: 30 minutes          Yield: 3 waffles (5x9 inches)

Judy Beemer
Sharon Springs, Kansas


# SUNDAY MORNING WAFFLES

1 3/4 c. unbleached flour
3 tsp. baking powder
1/2 tsp. salt
2 beaten egg yolks

1 3/4 c. milk
1/2 c. oil
1 Tbsp. fructose
2 stiffly beaten egg whites

Stir together first 3 ingredients. Combine yolks, milk and oil; stir into dry ingredients. Beat egg whites and add fructose. Fold whites into mixture, leaving a few fluffs. Bake in waffle iron.

Preparation time: 15 minutes          Yield: 8 (10-inch) waffles
   Hint: Try these variations:
1. Ham Waffles—sprinkle 2 tablespoons chopped cooked ham on each waffle before baking.
2. Cheese Waffles—stir in 3/4 cup grated Cheddar cheese in above mixture.
3. Pecan Waffles—sprinkle 2 tablespoons broken pecans atop waffles before baking.

Joe Sutton
Harrison, Arkansas

## WHOLE WHEAT WAFFLES

Heat iron while mixing batter.

| | |
|---|---|
| 2 eggs, beaten | 1/4 c. wheat germ |
| 2 c. sour milk | 2 tsp. baking powder |
| 1 tsp. soda | 1/2 tsp. salt |
| 1 3/4 c. whole wheat flour | 6 Tbsp. oil |

Combine all ingredients and beat until smooth. Bake in hot waffle iron and serve with honey-butter, fresh fruit, applesauce or favorite topping.

Preparation time: 30 minutes     Yield: Approximately 8 waffles
Hint: You can use all whole wheat flour (omit the wheat germ) or 1 cup whole wheat and 1 cup unbleached flour.

Cindy Mahan
Spokane, Washington


## BUTTERMILK WAFFLES

| | |
|---|---|
| 2 c. whole wheat flour | 2 1/2 c. buttermilk (or whole milk, |
| 1 Tbsp. baking powder | if desired) |
| 1 tsp. salt | 4 eggs, separated |
| 3/4 tsp. soda | 1/2 c. oil |

Sift dry ingredients twice, adding sifted bran and germ to the mixture. Add buttermilk, egg yolks and oil gradually, beating well; batter will be thin. Beat egg whites until stiff; fold into batter. Bake in preheated waffle iron.

Preparation time: 20-30 minutes     Yield: 4-6 servings

Shirley Nickels
Vancouver, Washington


## YOGURT PANCAKES

| | |
|---|---|
| 1 1/4 c. whole wheat flour | 1 c. plain yogurt |
| 1 tsp. soda | 2 eggs, separated |
| 1/2 tsp. salt | 2 Tbsp. oil |
| 1/2 tsp. baking powder | 2 Tbsp. honey |

Mix dry ingredients. Combine yogurt, egg yolks, oil and honey, then add to dry ingredients. Beat egg whites until stiff, then fold gently into batter. Bake on preheated oiled griddle and serve warm.

Preparation time: 25 minutes     Yield: 4-6 servings

Betty Vanderschaaf
Orange City, Iowa

## WHEAT GERM-BANANA PANCAKES

2 eggs
1 1/2 c. milk
1 large banana, mashed
1 (8 oz.) can crushed unsweetened
   pineapple, drained

1 c. unbleached flour
1/2 c. wheat germ
1 tsp. baking powder
1/2 tsp. salt
Additional wheat germ (optional)

Beat eggs in a small mixing bowl until foamy. Add milk, banana, and pineapple; beat well. Combine flour, wheat germ, baking powder, and salt in a bowl; stir well. Add the dry ingredients to the banana mixture, stirring just until moistened. For each pancake, pour 1/3 cup batter onto a hot, lightly greased griddle or skillet. Sprinkle with additional wheat germ, if desired. Turn pancakes when tops are covered with bubbles and edges look cooked. Serve pancakes hot with butter and honey or maple syrup.

Preparation time: 20 minutes     Yield: About 10 (5-inch) pancakes

Mrs. Penny Tutton
Leesburg, Florida

## OATMEAL PANCAKES

3/4 c. whole wheat flour
4 tsp. baking powder
1/2 tsp. salt
1 1/2 c. oats

2 eggs
1 Tbsp. oil
1 Tbsp. honey
1 1/4 c. milk

Mix dry ingredients. Combine eggs, oil, honey and milk. Add to dry ingredients, stirring until just moist. Bake on hot, lightly greased griddle.

Preparation time: 20 minutes     Yield: About 6 large pancakes

Hint: Combine and warm the following ingredients for a delicious syrup:

1/2 c. honey
1/4 c. butter

Raisins, as desired
1/4 tsp. ginger or cinnamon

Mary Lu Wheeler
Willard, Missouri

## OATMEAL-BUCKWHEAT PANCAKES

2 c. milk
1 1/2 c. oats
1 c. buckwheat or whole
    wheat flour

2 1/2 tsp. baking powder
1 tsp. salt
2 eggs, well beaten
1/3 c. oil

Pour milk over the oats and set aside for 5 minutes. Sift dry ingredients into a bowl, then stir in the oat mixture, eggs and oil. Blend until mixed well, then drop by 1/4 cup measure onto a lightly oiled hot griddle. Serve warm with honey and applesauce.

Preparation time: 20 minutes          Yield: 4 servings

Mrs. Charles F. Morgan
Knoxville, Tennessee

## REGAL PANCAKES

2 Tbsp. nutritional yeast
7/8 c. whole wheat flour
2 tsp. baking powder
3/4 c. milk

1 egg
2 Tbsp. honey
2 Tbsp. oil

Put the nutritional yeast in the bottom of a 1 cup measuring cup then fill with the flour. This is how you measure the 7/8 cup. Put this in a bowl with the baking powder; then mix in liquids and stir until moistened. Bake on an oiled griddle or skillet and turn when dry and bubbly on one side. Serve warm with butter and honey or maple syrup.

Preparation time: 10 minutes          Yield: 12-14 pancakes

Marcella Brown
Marcus, Iowa

## LIGHT PANCAKES

1/4 c. whole wheat flour
3/4 c. unbleached flour
1 1/2 tsp. baking powder
1/2 tsp. salt
1/2 tsp. soda

1 c. buttermilk
2 eggs, beaten
2 Tbsp. honey
1 Tbsp. oil
1 tsp. cinnamon (optional)

Mix dry ingredients. Combine the rest of the ingredients and stir into the dry mixture just until moistened. Cook on hot greased griddle, about 1 tablespoon per pancake, until bubbly; turn and cook until brown. Serve with applesauce or honey.

Preparation time: 10 minutes          Yield: Serves 3-4 people

Kris Wilson
Memphis, Tennessee

-14-

# VERY LIGHT PANCAKES

1 c. sifted unbleached or
   whole wheat flour
   (whole wheat makes a
   little heavier pancake)
2 Tbsp. baking powder

1/2 tsp. salt
1 c. milk
1 beaten egg
2 Tbsp. oil
2 Tbsp. honey

Sift together flour, baking powder, and salt. Combine remaining ingredients and add to flour mixture, beating until blended well. Bake on hot griddle.

Preparation time: 15 minutes      Yield: 8-10 small pancakes
   Hint: This recipe contains an unusually high amount of baking powder in proportion to the other ingredients. You may want to reduce it somewhat. Be sure and serve bananas, raisins or other high potassium foods with this recipe, especially if blood pressure is a problem.

Gloria Dooley
Wynne, Arkansas

# WHOLE WHEAT GERMAN PANCAKES OR CREPES

1 c. unsifted, unbleached flour
1/4 c. cornstarch
3 eggs

1 3/4 c. milk
1/2 tsp. salt
1 Tbsp. oil or melted butter

Put all ingredients in blender and blend until smooth. Heat a large fry pan; put enough oil in pan to coat, and have pan very hot. Tip and roll the pan in order to spread the batter thin and evenly. Brown quickly on one side and flip over. It takes a minute or two for the whole process.
   Put a small amount of your favorite filling in for pancakes and roll jelly roll fashion; then top with whipped cream sweetened with honey. (Example: Blueberry sauce as listed on page 88 of *Feasting Naturally....From Your Own Recipes,* topped with whipped cream.)
   Note: As crepes, fill with your favorite filling and roll up. Makes a change for your children or husband's lunchbox.

Preparation time: 10-12 minutes     Yield: 4-6 large or
                                 9 (7-inch) pancakes

Shirley Nickels
Vancouver, Washington

## BUTTERMILK PANCAKES

| | |
|---|---|
| 1 c. whole wheat flour | 1 c. buttermilk (or more for |
| 1/2 c. unbleached flour | thinner pancakes) |
| 1/2 c. wheat germ | 1 Tbsp. oil |
| 1 Tbsp. baking powder | Additional oil or shortening |
| 2 eggs | for griddle |

Preheat skillet or griddle with oil or vegetable shortening. Stir together flours, wheat germ, and baking powder. Add eggs, buttermilk, and 1 tablespoon oil. Stir just until moistened. Bake on preheated griddle. Serve with butter and honey.

Preparation time: 20 minutes          Yield: 6-8 pancakes
   Hint: Salt and baking soda have been purposely omitted.

Mrs. Vernon Dunn
St. Charles, Missouri

## OAT SCONES

| | |
|---|---|
| 1 3/4 c. oats | 1 tsp. lecithin granules |
| 1 1/4 c. whole wheat flour | 5 Tbsp. butter (part oil, if desired) |
| 1/2 tsp. soda | 1 egg |
| Dash salt | Buttermilk or homemade yogurt |

Mix oats, flour, soda, salt and lecithin. Cut in butter. Beat egg and add enough buttermilk to make one cup. Add to dry ingredients, mixing with fork. On buttered cookie sheet, divide dough into 3 parts; using fork make into flat rounds 1/2 inch thick. Bake at 375 degrees for 15-20 minutes until lightly browned.

Preparation time: 30 minutes          Yield: 3 scones

Helen Galloway
Big Sandy, Texas

## CHEESE CRACKERS

| | |
|---|---|
| 3/4 c. whole wheat flour | 1/3 c. butter or margarine, softened |
| 1/4 c. wheat germ | 1 1/2 c. shredded Cheddar cheese |
| 1/4 tsp. salt | (sharp or medium) |

Combine flour, wheat germ and salt. Add butter and cheese and mix with hand to form dough. Divide in half. Shape each half in a roll, 1 1/2 inches in diameter. Wrap in plastic wrap and chill until very firm—about 1 hour. Cut with serrated knife in very thin slices. Bake on a lightly greased cookie sheet, 350 degree oven, 12-14 minutes, or until golden brown. Remove and cool on rack. Store in airtight container in cool, dry place. Will keep about 2 weeks.

Preparation time: 1 1/2 hours          Yield: 3 dozen

Cindy Mahan
Spokane, Washington

## CORN TORTILLAS

2 c. milk
1 c. stone ground yellow
corn meal
1 c. unbleached flour (can use
whole wheat, but texture is
not as good)

2 beaten eggs
5 Tbsp. cornstarch
1 tsp. salt
2 Tbsp. oil

Place all ingredients except oil in blender or food processor and blend well. Put oil in a very large hot frying pan. Put a small amount of batter in center of pan. Then tip and tilt the pan until the batter is very thin and covers the whole pan. When it is browned, flip to the other side. (The whole process only takes a couple of minutes.)

Stack tortillas on top of each other, wrap in oiled paper then cloth or foil to keep moist. Refrigerate if not used at once.

Preparation time: 30 minutes          Yield: 20 tortillas

Shirley Nickels
Vancouver, Washington


## COUNTRY FRESH BISCUITS

6 c. unbleached flour
1/2 c. powdered milk
1/4 c. baking powder
2 tsp. salt

2 tsp. cream of tartar
1 Tbsp. fructose
2 c. shortening, butter or
margarine
1 1/2 c. water

Blend all ingredients, except shortening and water, to resemble coarse crumbs. Cut in shortening with pastry blender. Stir in water until moistened. Turn onto floured surface. Knead 8-10 times until smooth. Roll dough 3/4" thick. Cut with cookie cutter and place biscuits on cookie sheet. Bake 20 minutes at 400 degrees.

Preparation time: 30 minutes          Yield: 2 dozen biscuits
Hint: To Freeze - Place cut out biscuits on cookie sheet, cover and freeze. Remove frozen biscuits and put in plastic bag to store in freezer. Preheat oven to 400 degrees. Bake frozen biscuits on cookie sheet for 30-35 minutes until golden.

Rona Speropolous
DeSoto, Missouri

# SOURDOUGH STARTER

2 c. unbleached flour                    2 Tbsp. honey
2 c. lukewarm water                      1 pkg. dry yeast

Mix in large glass or plastic bowl. Cover with a cloth. Leave on kitchen counter for 3 days, stirring occasionally. Refrigerate loosely covered so that fermentation gasses can escape.
(Always keep at least one cup of the starter.)
Before you bake, remove from refrigerator, add equal amounts of flour and water, and stir. Leave out overnight in warm spot. Replenishing this way will insure always having enough to use and keep for next time.

Preparation time: 5 minutes          Yield: 2 cups

Kris Wilson
Memphis, Tennessee

# SOURDOUGH BISCUITS

2 c. unbleached flour                    1/3 c. powdered milk
  (or) 1 3/4 c. unbleached flour         1 c. sourdough starter
  and 1/4 c. wheat germ                  4 Tbsp. oil
1/2 tsp. salt                            1/2 c. warm water
1/2 tsp. soda

Mix dry ingredients; combine moist ingredients, add to the dry ingredients. Dough should hold together; if not, add a little water. Knead about 1 minute on surface sprinkled with unbleached flour. Roll 1/2 inch thick and cut with a 2-inch biscuit cutter. Bake at 450 degrees about 10-15 minutes, until lightly browned.

Preparation time: 20 minutes         Yield: About one dozen

Kris Wilson
Memphis, Tennessee

# LIGHT CORN MEAL CRESCENTS

1 Tbsp. yeast
1/2 c. warm water
1 1/2 c. lukewarm milk
1 c. yellow corn meal
1/4 c. honey

1/2 c. softened butter
2 eggs, slightly beaten
2 tsp. salt
5 3/4 - 6 1/2 c. unbleached flour

Dissolve yeast in warm water. Stir in milk, corn meal, honey, butter, eggs, salt and 2 cups of flour. Beat, then stir in enough flour to make dough easy to handle. Knead 5 minutes; cover and let rise 1 1/2 hours. Grease 2 baking sheets; sprinkle with corn meal. Punch dough down and divide in half. Roll each half in circle, then spread with butter. Cut into 16 wedges, roll up and place on baking sheet. Let rise 40 minutes. Brush with melted butter, then sprinkle with corn meal and bake 15-20 minutes in 400 degree oven.

Preparation time: 45 minutes + rising time

Yield: 16 rolls

Jackie Kelsey
Mt. Carmel, Illinois

# WHOLE EARTH MUFFINS

1/2 c. wheat germ
1 c. whole wheat flour
1/2 c. unbleached flour
1 1/2 tsp. soda
1/2 c. raisins

1/4 - 1/2 c. honey (depends on individual taste)
8 oz. plain yogurt
2 eggs
1/4 c. oil

Combine wheat germ, flours, soda, and raisins. Mix honey, yogurt, eggs and oil and pour over dry ingredients. Stir quickly and lightly to moisten dry ingredients. Do not beat. Spoon into greased or paper-lined 2 1/2-inch muffin cups, filling 3/4 full. Bake in 400 degree oven for 15 minutes or until done.

Preparation time: 20-25 minutes

Yield: 12 muffins

Jan Castor
Plainfield, Indiana

## OATMEAL BANANA MUFFINS

1/2 c. butter
2 eggs
2-3 bananas, mashed
1/2 c. honey

1/4 c. plain yogurt (or peach
  is good)
1 tsp. soda
1 1/2 c. whole wheat flour
1 c. oats

Blend the butter, eggs, bananas and honey. Add the yogurt and soda. Cream well. Add the flour and oats and mix well. Fill 18-20 muffin cups 2/3 full. Bake at 375 degrees for 18-20 minutes. Remove from pans and cool on wire rack. These freeze well.

Preparation time: 25 minutes          Yield: 1 1/2 dozen

Carole Jasinek
San Diego, California

## BANANA-HONEY MUFFINS

3/4 c. whole wheat flour
3/4 c. unbleached flour
2 tsp. baking powder
1/2 tsp. salt
3/4 c. oats

1 egg
3/4 c. milk
1 medium banana, mashed
1/4 c. oil
1/4 c. honey

Add dry ingredients to wet ingredients. Stir until moist and fill paper lined muffin cups 2/3 full. Bake at 400 degrees for 15 minutes.

Preparation time: 30 minutes          Yield: 18 muffins

Betsy Branstetter
Kansas City, Missouri

## BLUEBERRY MUFFINS

1 egg
3/4 c. plain yogurt
2 Tbsp. oil
1/4 c. honey

1/4 tsp. salt
1 tsp. soda
1 1/2 c. whole wheat flour
1/2 - 1 c. fresh or frozen blueberries

Mix the first four ingredients. Stir in salt, soda, and flour. Gently fold in blueberries. Bake the muffins for 30 minutes at 350 degrees. Be sure to butter and flour the pan well or use paper cups. Grease the pan with butter or lecithin and dust with whole wheat flour.

Preparation time: 40 minutes          Yield: 12 muffins
     Hint: Best results are obtained with 1/2 cup blueberries. Look for frozen variety in your area packaged without sugar, if fresh are not available.

Mary J. Steffens
Marcus, Iowa

## GLORIA'S BLUEBERRY MUFFINS

3 Tbsp. oil
6 Tbsp. honey
1 c. milk
1 egg, beaten
1 c. whole wheat flour

1 c. unbleached flour
1 Tbsp. baking powder
1/2 tsp. salt
1/2 c. blueberries

Combine oil, honey , milk and egg; mix well. Add dry mixture to the liquids stirring only enough to mix. Fold in blueberries; fill muffin tins 2/3 full with batter and bake for 20-25 minutes at 400 degrees until lightly browned.

Preparation time: 40 minutes          Yield: 12 muffins

Gloria Dooley
Wynne, Arkansas

## BLUEBERRY MUFFINS ala KATHLEEN

1 2/3 c. whole wheat flour
2 1/4 tsp. baking powder
1 tsp. salt
1-3 Tbsp. fructose

1 beaten egg
1 1/3 c. milk
4 Tbsp. melted butter
1/2 - 1 c. blueberries, fresh
        or frozen

Mix together flour, baking powder, salt and fructose. Beat egg until light; add milk and slightly cooled butter. Toss in flour mixture and stir quickly just enough to dampen flour. Fold in blueberries. Let stand a few minutes until mixture thickens, then drop by teaspoonfuls into muffin tins and bake at 425 degrees for 20-25 minutes.

Preparation time: 40 minutes          Yield: 12 muffins

Kathleen Hackman
London, Arkansas

## HONEY MUFFINS

1 egg
1 c. milk
1/4 c. oil
1/2 c. honey

1 1/2 c. unbleached flour
2 tsp. baking powder
1/2 tsp. salt
1/2 c. chopped pecans

Beat egg, add milk and oil. Mix well. Slowly blend in honey. Sift dry ingredients together. In center of flour add milk, eggs, honey and oil mixture. Stir quickly until moist, add pecans. Fill greased or paper lined muffin tin two-thirds full. Bake at about 425 degrees for 20 minutes.

Preparation time: 30-40 minutes          Yield: 12 muffins

Virginia McWilliams
Atlanta, Texas

# RAISIN MUFFINS

1 c. raisins
1 c. water
1/2 c. butter
3/4 c. honey
1 egg

1 3/4 c. unbleached flour
1 tsp. salt
1 tsp. nutmeg
1 tsp. soda

Boil raisins for 15 minutes in water. Meanwhile, cream butter and honey thoroughly, then add egg. Add dry ingredients; beat until mixed. Add raisins and 1/2 cup of the raisin liquid. Blend thoroughly, then pour into paper lined or oiled muffin tins. Bake at 325 degrees about 15 minutes.

Preparation time: 30 minutes          Yield: About 2 dozen
Hint: Save extra raisin liquid if there is any, and use as a sweetener. Recipe is also good using all whole wheat flour or half whole wheat and half unbleached.

Marsha Hills
Peace River, Alberta, Canada


# BRAN MUFFINS

1 c. unbleached flour
2 Tbsp. wheat germ
2 Tbsp. bran
1/4 tsp. baking powder
1 tsp. soda
1/4 c. oil

1/4 c. honey
1 egg
1/2 c. milk
1 c. grated zucchini
1/4 c. sunflower seeds

Combine flour, wheat germ, bran, baking powder and soda in a large bowl. In a small bowl, combine oil, honey, egg, and milk. Add liquid ingredients to dry ones. Stir in zucchini, sunflower seeds. Spoon into buttered or paper-lined muffin tins, filling them about 2/3 full. Bake at 325 degrees for 25-30 minutes.

Preparation time: 35 minutes          Yield: 12-14 muffins
Hint: For microwave cooking: Add all ingredients at once in a food processor, then mix. Fill paper lined microwave muffin pan. Microwave six at a time on high power for 1 minute, 20 seconds; take out and place on flat surface.

Diane Ruden
Marcus, Iowa

# REFRIGERATOR BRAN MUFFINS

| | |
|---|---|
| 1 c. wheat germ | 2 1/2 c. whole wheat flour |
| 1 c. boiling water | 1 tsp. salt |
| 1 1/2 c. honey | 3 tsp. soda |
| 1/2 c. oil | 1 c. buttermilk |
| 2 eggs | 2 c. bran |

Mix wheat germ with boiling water. Let cool. Cream honey and oil; add eggs, mixing in one at a time. Add flour, salt, and soda alternately with buttermilk. Last of all add wheat germ and bran. Mix well. Refrigerate batter at least one day. Bake in paper lined muffin tins for 20 minutes at 400 degrees. This mixture can be kept refrigerated for several weeks.

Preparation time: 15 minutes         Yield: About 1 1/2 qt. mix

Janet Hillstrand
Harlan, Iowa


# TASTY MUFFINS

| | |
|---|---|
| 3/4 c. milk | 1 c. rolled oats |
| 3/4 c. bran | 2/3 c. unbleached wheat flour |
| 1 egg | 1 Tbsp. baking powder |
| 1/4 c. oil | 1/4 tsp. soda |
| 1/4 c. honey | 1/4 tsp. salt, if desired |
| 1/4 c. fructose | |

Combine milk and bran in bowl adding egg, oil, honey and fructose, mixing well. Add remaining ingredients, mixing until dry ingredients are just moist. Fill 12 greased or paper lined muffin cups 2/3 full. Bake in preheated oven at 400 degrees for 15 minutes.

Preparation time: 30 minutes         Yield: 12 muffins
    Hint: Microwave directions: Use 2 tablespoons more oil and fill paper cups only 1/2 full. Microwave on high for 30 seconds and rotate, microwave 30 seconds. Check for doneness; if not done, bake 30 seconds more. Remove and bake the rest. Makes 18 muffins.

Lona Yender
Nemaha, Iowa

# WHOLE WHEAT MUFFINS

| | |
|---|---|
| 2 1/2 c. whole wheat flour | 1 c. buttermilk |
| 2 Tbsp. baking powder | 1/2 c. honey (scant) |
| 1/2 tsp. soda | 1 egg, slightly beaten |
| 1/8 tsp. salt | 2 Tbsp. safflower oil |

Combine dry ingredients in a bowl and make a well in the center. Add wet ingredients and stir just until moistened. Fill greased muffin tins 2/3 full and bake at 425 degrees for 15 minutes.

Preparation time: 20 minutes        Yield: 12 muffins
    Hint: Vary muffins by adding nuts or seeds, fruits, carob, etc.

Genevieve Russell
Dallas, Texas

# CORN MUFFINS (SALT FREE)

| | |
|---|---|
| 1/2 c. unbleached flour | 1/4 tsp. potassium chloride |
| 1/2 c. stone ground yellow | 1 c. buttermilk |
| corn meal | 2 Tbsp. melted butter, margarine |
| 1 tsp. low sodium baking powder | or oil |
| | 1 egg |

Preheat oven to 450 degrees, then oil 6 muffin tins and place in oven. Combine dry ingredients, then add buttermilk, butter and egg. Mix well, then pour into hot muffin tins and bake for 10-15 minutes.

Preparation time: 20 minutes        Yield: 6 muffins
    Hint: Low sodium baking powder can be found in specialty stores; potassium chloride, a salt substitute, can be found in drug stores.

Mrs. E.C. Shackleford
Hollandale, Mississippi

# WHOLE WHEAT CORN BREAD

| | |
|---|---|
| 1 c. stone ground corn meal | 1/2 tsp. salt |
| 1 c. whole wheat flour | 1 c. milk |
| 1 Tbsp. fructose or honey | 1/4 c. oil |
| 4 tsp. baking powder | 1 egg |

Mix dry ingredients in large bowl and set aside. In small bowl beat milk, oil and egg with fork until blended. Add to dry mixture and stir just to moisten. Bake in 8-inch square pan in preheated 425 degree oven for 20-25 minutes. Cut in squares and serve hot.

Preparation time: 35 minutes        Yield: 9 servings

Genevieve Russell
Dallas, Texas

# CAROL'S CORN BREAD

| | |
|---|---|
| 1 1/2 c. stone ground yellow<br>   corn meal | 1/2 tsp. salt<br>1/4 c. honey |
| 1 c. whole wheat flour | 1 egg |
| 4 tsp. baking powder | 1/4 c. oil |
| | 1 c. milk |

Sift together dry ingredients. Add honey, egg, oil and milk. Beat about 1 minute, until smooth. Bake in buttered 8-inch square or round pan at 400 degrees for 20-25 minutes.

Preparation time: 35 minutes     Yield: 8-10 servings (leftovers can be refrigerated and reheated)

Hint: I add the bran back into the batter after sifting.

Carol Mehegan
West Plains, Missouri

# CAROL'S HONEY CORN BREAD

| | |
|---|---|
| 1 c. yellow corn meal | 2 eggs, beaten |
| 3/4 c. unbleached flour | 3/4 c. milk |
| 4 tsp. baking powder | 1/4 c. honey |
| 3/4 tsp. salt | 2 Tbsp. oil |

Preheat oven to 425 degrees; oil an 8-inch square baking dish thoroughly. Mix ingredients in a bowl using an electric mixer on low speed. Bake 15 minutes.

Preparation time: 20 minutes     Yield: 16 pieces

Carol Ashberry
Cabot, Arkansas

# JANET'S CORN BREAD

| | |
|---|---|
| 1 c. stone ground yellow<br>   corn meal (ground fine<br>   in blender) | 1/4 c. honey<br>4 tsp. baking powder<br>1 egg |
| 1/2 c. whole wheat flour | 1 c. milk |
| 1/2 c. unbleached flour | 1/4 c. oil |
| 1/2 tsp. salt | |

Mix dry ingredients. Add honey, egg, milk and oil, beating just until blended. Bake at 425 degrees for 20-25 minutes in an oiled 9-inch square pan.

Preparation time: 45 minutes     Yield: 8 servings

Hint: Double recipe for a 13x9 inch pan.

Janet Campbell
Corvallis, Oregon

# CORN BREAD

3/4 c. stone ground yellow
  corn meal
1 c. unbleached flour
2 Tbsp. fructose
1 tsp. salt

1 Tbsp. baking powder
1 egg
2/3 c. milk
1/3 c. oil or melted butter

Mix first 5 ingredients well. Combine egg, milk, and oil. Add to dry ingredients and mix well with a spoon. Bake at 425 degrees for 25 minutes in an oiled 8-inch square pan.

Preparation time: 45 minutes     Yield: 6-8 servings

Claudia Tanner
Eaton Rapids, Michigan

## BUTTERMILK CORN BREAD

2 Tbsp. butter or margarine
1 c. whole wheat flour
1 c. stone ground yellow
  corn meal
1/2 c. wheat germ

1 Tbsp. baking powder
2 Tbsp. honey
1 egg
1 c. buttermilk (a little more
  if needed)

Melt butter in oven in a cast iron skillet at 350 degrees. Combine flour, corn meal, wheat germ and baking powder in a bowl. Add honey, egg, buttermilk and melted butter. Stir until moistened and return mixture to heated skillet. Bake 15 minutes or until done at 350 degrees.

Preparation time: 20-25 minutes     Yield: 6 servings

Mrs. Vernon Dunn
St. Charles, Missouri

## DATE NUT BREAD

1 c. dates
1/2 c. nuts
1/2 c. raisins
2 Tbsp. butter

1 tsp. soda
1 c. boiling water
1 egg
1 c. whole wheat flour

Butter an 8x4 inch loaf pan. Chop dates and nuts coarsely and combine with raisins, butter, and soda in a mixing bowl. Pour boiling water over all and stir. Allow to cool to lukewarm, then stir in the egg. Add the flour, mixing thoroughly with a spatula or wooden spoon. Pour batter into the prepared pan and bake at 350 degrees until done, 1 - 1 1/2 hours.

Preparation time: 2 hours     Yield: 1 loaf

Janet E. Griffin
Grand Junction, Colorado

# BOSTON BROWN BREAD

1 c. honey
2 c. buttermilk or
    plain yogurt
3 c. whole wheat flour
1/2 c. wheat germ
1 tsp. baking powder
1 tsp. soda
Dash salt

1 c. sunflower seeds
1 c. raisins
1/2 c. chopped prunes
1/2 c. chopped dates
1/2 c. chopped pecans or
    walnuts
1/3 c. unhulled sesame seeds

Mix honey and buttermilk or yogurt. Combine flour, wheat germ, baking powder, soda and salt. Add to liquids, reserving 3 tablespoons flour mixture. Dredge remaining ingredients in reserved flour mixture and mix into batter. Pour into buttered cans, (#2 size is nice), filling only half full. Cover slightly with foil and bake at 350 degrees for 55 minutes. Allow to cool in cans for 10 minutes before removing; finish cooling on wire racks.

Preparation time: 1 1/2 hours        Yield: 4-6 round loaves

Helen Galloway
Big Sandy, Texas

# HONEY DATE NUT BREAD

3/4 c. boiling water
1 c. pitted whole dates, chopped
1 egg
1 c. honey
1 Tbsp. soft butter

1 tsp. vanilla
2 c. whole wheat flour
1 tsp. soda
1 c. chopped walnuts
1/2 tsp. salt

Pour 3/4 cup boiling water over dates and let stand until cool. Don't drain. Beat egg until thick and light. Beat in honey, butter and vanilla. Stir undrained dates into egg mixture. Stir together flour, soda and salt. By hand, carefully stir flour mixture into egg mixture along with nuts just until combined. Pour batter into two greased 7 1/2 x 3 1/2 x 2-inch loaf pans or one greased 9x5x3-inch loaf pan. Bake at 350 degrees for 50 minutes for small pans or 65 minutes for large pan. Cool in pans for 10 minutes. Remove and cool completely on wire racks.

Preparation time: 1 1/2 hours        Yield: 2 small or 1 large loaf

Cathy Bodell
Fullerton, California

# DATE NUT LOAF

| | |
|---|---|
| 1 1/2 c. boiling water | 2 1/4 c. unbleached flour |
| 1 c. chopped dates | 2 tsp. soda |
| 1 c. honey | 1/2 tsp. salt |
| 1 beaten egg | 1/4 tsp. baking powder |
| 1 tsp. oil | 3/4 c. walnut pieces |
| 1 tsp. vanilla | |

Pour boiling water over dates and allow to stand for 10 minutes. Meanwhile, beat together the honey, egg, oil and vanilla. Sift flour, baking soda, salt and baking powder together being careful to add the bran back to the sifted mixture. Add this sifted mixture to honey mixture and beat until well mixed. Add dates, mix well, then add walnuts. Pour into a well-greased loaf pan and bake for 1 hour at 275 degrees. Loaf will spring back in center when done.

Preparation time: 1 hour 15 minutes   Yield: 1 loaf
Hint: Send this bread sliced thin with cheese and accompanied by celery and carrot sticks for a delicious lunch.

Marsha Hills
Peace River, Alberta, Canada

# WHOLE WHEAT HONEY NUT BREAD

| | |
|---|---|
| 1 c. whole wheat flour | 1 tsp. salt |
| 1 1/4 c. unbleached flour | 3 Tbsp. oil |
| 1/4 c. wheat germ | 1 1/4 c. milk |
| 1 c. honey | 1 egg |
| 3 1/2 tsp. baking powder | 1 c. chopped nuts |

Measure all ingredients into a large bowl; beat on medium speed until well blended. Pour mixture into greased and floured 9x5-inch pan. Bake at 350 degrees for one hour or until toothpick inserted in center comes out clean. To cook in microwave, pour mixture into microwave designed tube pan. Simmer for 9 minutes, then cook on high for 5 1/2 minutes or until toothpick inserted near center comes out clean.

Preparation time: 10 minutes +        Yield: 1 loaf
                  one hour in oven
            (14 1/2 minutes in microwave)
Hint: This freezes well and makes a nice gift. It's great heated for breakfast and topped with butter, peanut butter, or homemade jelly.

Rebecca Hare
Swartz, Louisiana

## PUMPKIN BREAD

1 c. canned pumpkin
1 c. honey
2 eggs
1/2 c. oil
2 c. unbleached flour

1 tsp. soda
1/2 tsp. salt
1 1/2 tsp. pumpkin pie spice
1/2 c. raisins
1/2 c. nuts

Put pumpkin, honey, eggs, and oil in blender. Blend until smooth. In mixing bowl, stir together the flour, soda, salt and spice. Add the pumpkin mixture, raisins and nuts. Stir to mix. Pour into a buttered 9x5-inch loaf pan. Bake at 350 degrees for about 70 minutes or until bread tests done. Remove from pan and cool on rack.

Preparation time: 1 1/2 hours        Yield: 1 loaf

Betty Ritter
St. Marys, Missouri

## BANANA BREAD

2 c. unbleached flour
1 tsp. soda
1/4 tsp. salt
1 c. honey
1/2 c. butter or margarine

2 eggs, lightly beaten
1/4 c. buttermilk
3 ripe bananas, mashed
1/2 c. nuts, chopped
1/2 c. raisins

Sift dry ingredients, adding bran back to mixture. Warm honey, and cream with butter; add eggs and buttermilk, then bananas; beat until smooth. Add dry ingredients and beat only until mixed; stir in nuts and raisins and pour into a well-greased 9x5-inch loaf pan. Bake at 350 degrees for 1 hour.

Preparation time: 1 1/2 hours        Yield: 1 loaf

Mary Lois Johnsey
Water Valley, Mississippi

## MIRANDA'S BREAD

2 c. whole wheat flour
2/3 c. honey
1 tsp. soda
1 pinch salt

1 egg
1 c. buttermilk
2 Tbsp. oil

Mix with spoon in bowl. Pour into lightly greased loaf pan. Bake at 350 degrees for 40-50 minutes.

Preparation time: 1 hour        Yield: 15-20 slices

Miranda Brown
Knoxville, Tennessee

## EARLY AMERICAN HERB BREAD

1 c. whole wheat flour
2/3 c. unbleached flour
1/3 c. soy or rye flour
1/2 tsp. salt
1 1/2 tsp. baking powder
1/2 tsp. soda

1/2 tsp. basil
1/4 tsp. oregano
1/8 tsp. thyme
1 egg
2/3 c. buttermilk
2 Tbsp. honey
1 Tbsp. oil

Sift all dry ingredients. Beat egg, milk, honey and oil in separate bowl. Stir into dry ingredients. Add flour, if necessary, to knead lightly. Shape into plump disk. Cut 1/4 inch deep cross on top. Place on greased pan. Bake 30-40 minutes at 350 degrees.

Preparation time: 1 hour          Yield: 1 loaf

Mrs. Robert Hunt
Knoxville, Tennessee

## BUTTERMILK BREAD

5 1/2 - 6 1/2 c. flour (mixture
  of half unbleached and half
  whole wheat)
3 Tbsp. honey
2 1/2 tsp. soda

1 tsp. salt
1 pkg. yeast
3/4 c. buttermilk
3/4 c. water
1/3 c. butter

Mix buttermilk, water, butter and honey in saucepan and heat until warm. Mixture will appear curdled. Add mixture gradually to a mix of 2 cups flour, salt, soda and yeast. Add 1 cup flour or enough to make a thick batter. Beat at high speed 2 minutes. Stir in 2 1/2 cups more flour to make dough soft; knead 10 minutes. Cover and let rise until double; punch down. Make 2 loaves in 8 1/2 x 4 1/2 inch pans. Cover with a moist towel and let rise until double.
Bake at 375 degrees for 35 minutes. Remove from pans immediately. Rub butter on tops; cool on wire racks.

Preparation time: 3 hours          Yield: 2 loaves

Cheryl Patrick
Harrison, Arkansas

# BASIC YEAST BREAD
## (Variations included)

| | |
|---|---|
| 2 c. milk | 1/3 c. honey |
| 3 Tbsp. oil | 2 pkg. yeast |
| 1 tsp. salt | 5 - 5 1/2 c. unbleached flour |

Heat milk to simmer. Add oil, salt and honey to milk and pour into large mixing bowl and cool to lukewarm. Dissolve yeast in 1/3 cup lukewarm water and add to milk mixture. Mix on low speed of mixer and add 3 cups flour. Beat for 6 minutes on medium speed. Add 2 more cups flour by kneading it on floured surface. Knead more flour if necessary to make dough smooth and elastic. Place in oiled bowl and cover. Let rise in a warm place until doubled. Knead down to original size, cut in half, and shape into two loaves. Cover and let rise until dough reaches the top of the pan. Bake at 375 degrees for 35-45 minutes (until golden brown).

## Variations:

1. Herb bread - add to milk mixture any of the following:

   | | |
   |---|---|
   | 4 tsp. leaf sage | 4 tsp. parsley flakes |
   | 4 tsp. caraway seeds | 4 tsp. poppy seeds as desired |

2. Whole wheat - replace last 2 cups flour with 2 cups whole wheat (a very dark bread can be made by using whole wheat flour entirely - although the bread doesn't rise as well).

3. Rye bread - replace 2 cups flour with rye flour and 2 1/2 cups flour with whole wheat flour; add unbleached flour for remaining flour. Add 3 tablespoons caraway seeds.

Preparation time: 3 hours          Yield: 2 loaves

Lou Sutton
Harrison, Arkansas

## OATMEAL BREAD

| | |
|---|---|
| 1 3/4 c. boiling water | 2 pkg. yeast |
| 1 c. oats | 1/2 c. warm water |
| 1 Tbsp. salt | 5 c. unbleached flour |
| 2 Tbsp. oil | 1 egg yolk |
| 1/2 c. honey | Poppy seeds |

Pour boiling water over one cup oats. Let mixture stand for 1/2 hour. Stir in salt, oil, honey, and yeast which has been dissolved in 1/2 cup warm water, then add 5 cups unbleached flour (that has been warmed in 250 degree oven for 10 minutes). Add flour 1/2 cup at a time. When flour is all mixed in, knead dough for 7-10 minutes. (Add additional flour as needed to keep from sticking).

Place kneaded mixture in a lightly oiled bowl. Turn mixture to oil top. Cover with a cloth moistened with warm water. Place in oven with pilot light on or oven light on (if electric range). Place a pan of hot water under the rack that is holding the kneaded dough. Let rise until double, about 1 hour. When dough has doubled in size punch down and divide into two loaves. Knead each loaf for 1 minute to press out air bubbles. Shape into loaf shape and place in buttered 8 1/2 x 4 1/2 inch pans. Score top and along one side of top with a sharp knife. Mix an egg yolk with a few drops of water and brush on top of loaves. Sprinkle the tops of loaves with poppy seeds. Let rise for 30-45 minutes.

Bake in 325 degree oven for 40-50 minutes (depending on size of bread pans). If the top of the bread is browning too quickly, during the last few minutes of baking time cover with brown paper. When done, turn out onto wire rack and cool.

Preparation time: 3 hours          Yield: 2 loaves
    Hint: This bread makes delicious toast.

Judy Harned
Coyle, Oklahoma

## SHREDDED WHEAT BREAD

| | |
|---|---|
| 2 shredded wheat biscuits | 1 tsp. salt |
| (large) | 2 c. boiling water |
| 2 Tbsp. butter | 1 pkg. yeast |
| 2/3 c. honey | 6 c. unbleached flour |

Combine wheat biscuits, butter, honey and salt. Add water; cool. Dissolve yeast in 1/4 cup warm water. Add to biscuit mixture. Stir in flour with heavy spoon or spatula. Don't knead. Let rise overnight (or for 8 hours). Cut or punch down. Don't knead. Place in 2 loaf pans. Let rise until double (1 hour). Bake 45 minutes at 350 degrees. Remove from pans and cool.

Preparation time: 15 minutes plus     Yield: 2 loaves
              baking and rising time
    Hint: This recipe may be doubled successfully, freezes well, and has enough body to be sliced thinly for sandwiches. Despite the ease in preparation, the loaves are light and high. I find it an all around excellent bread.

## HONEY WHOLE WHEAT BREAD

1 pkg. active dry yeast
1/4 c. warm water (105 - 115 degrees)
2 c. cold water
1 c. powdered milk
1 c. honey
1/2 c. oil
1/4 c. wheat germ
2 tsp. salt
1 1/2 c. whole wheat flour
5 1/2 c. unbleached flour

In 5-quart bowl dissolve yeast in warm water; let stand 5 minutes. Add cold water, milk powder, honey, oil, wheat germ and salt; stir well. Add whole wheat flour; stir well. Gradually add about 5 cups flour, stirring well after each addition so no flour pockets remain. (Dough should look and feel as if ready to knead.) Cover well with plastic wrap; let stand in cool draft free place 8 to 14 hours. Sprinkle top of dough with 1/4 cup unbleached flour. Scrape down sides of bowl, turn dough out onto floured surface. Flatten with fingers. Work in dry spots; dust moist spots with flour. Roll up dough and knead until smooth and satiny. Divide in half; shape each half to fit greased 9x5x3-inch loaf pan. Cover and let rise until doubled in warm draft free place. Bake in 375 degree oven 1 hour or until loaves sound hollow when tapped.

Preparation time: 30 minutes plus rising time and baking time
Yield: 2 loaves
Hint: You may want to use less honey.

Annette Gerdes
Everton, Arkansas


## SUE'S WHOLE WHEAT BREAD

1 c. warm water
2 Tbsp. yeast
1 c. scalded milk, cooled
1/3 c. honey
1/4 c. oil
2 tsp. salt
2 beaten eggs, room temperature
5 1/2 - 6 c. whole wheat flour
(can use 4 1/2 c. whole wheat and 1 1/2 c. unbleached)

In mixing bowl, dissolve yeast in water. Add milk, honey, oil, salt and eggs. Stir in 2 1/2 cups flour and beat with electric mixer 3-4 minutes. Cover this sponge and let rise until double. Mix in remaining flour, reserving 1/2 cup for kneading. Knead 10-15 minutes. Let rise until double. Punch down and let rest 10 minutes. Shape into 2 loaves on floured surface. Place in greased bread pans, and let rise until double. Bake at 375 degrees for 40 minutes.

Preparation time: 3 1/2 hours
Yield: 2 loaves

Sue Riddle
Republic, Missouri

# HONEY OF A BREAD

| | |
|---|---|
| 3 1/2 - 4 c. unbleached flour | 1 c. water |
| 2 1/2 c. whole wheat flour | 1/2 c. honey |
| 2 pkg. dry yeast | 3 Tbsp. oil |
| 1 Tbsp. salt | 1 egg, room temperature |
| 1 c. milk | |

In large mixer bowl, combine 1 cup unbleached flour, whole wheat flour, yeast and salt; mix well. In saucepan, heat milk, water, honey and oil until warm; add to flour mixture. Add egg. Blend at low speed until moistened; beat 3 minutes at medium speed. By hand, gradually stir in remaining unbleached flour to make a firm dough. Knead on floured surface until smooth and elastic, about 5 minutes. Place in greased bowl, turning to grease top. Cover; let rise in warm place until light and doubled, about 1 hour. Punch down dough. Divide into 2 parts. On lightly floured surface, roll or pat each half to a 14x7-inch rectangle. Starting with the shorter side, roll up tightly, pressing dough into roll with each turn. Pinch edges and ends to seal. Place in greased (oiled) 9x5-inch loaf pans. Cover; let rise in warm place until light and doubled, about 30 minutes. Bake at 350 degrees for 25-30 minutes until golden brown. Remove from pans; cool.

Preparation time: 3 hours          Yield: 2 loaves

Ruth Ann Peters
Harrison, Arkansas

# JERRIE'S WHEAT BREAD

| | |
|---|---|
| 2 pkg. yeast | 6 c. whole wheat flour |
| 4 c. warm water | 4 eggs, room temperature |
| 1/3 c. bran | 6 Tbsp. butter or margarine |
| 1/2 c. honey | 2 Tbsp. salt |
| 1 c. oats | 5-6 c. unbleached flour |

Soften yeast in warm water. Add bran, honey, and oats. Stir in enough whole wheat flour to make a soft dough. Add eggs, butter and salt. Mix well. Add unbleached flour to make a soft dough, then knead in flour until dough is stiff and elastic. Place in greased bowl, turning to grease top. Cover and let rise until double. Punch dough down and put into greased loaf pans. Cover and let rise until double. Bake at 350 degrees for 35 minutes.

Preparation time: 3 - 3 1/2 hours     Yield: 3 short or 2 long loaves

Jerrie Altenbern
DeBeque, Colorado

# MICROWAVE WHEAT BREAD

1 large potato, peeled
  (about 1 1/2 c.)
1/2 c. water
1 1/4 c. water
1/2 c. wheat bran
1/2 c. stone ground corn meal
1/4 c. honey
2 Tbsp. butter or margarine

2 1/2 tsp. salt
1/4 c. warm water
1 Tbsp. yeast
3 to 3 1/2 c. unsifted unbleached
  flour
2 c. unsifted whole wheat flour
Toasted wheat germ

    Cut potato into 1 inch cubed pieces. Place in 1 1/2 quart casserole pan plus 1/2 cup water. Cover with plastic wrap. Microwave on high 4 1/2 to 5 minutes. Let stand, covered. Microwave on High 1 1/4 cups water in 1 1/2 quart casserole pan for 2 1/2 to 3 minutes or until boiling. Mash potato mixture. Add bran, corn meal, honey, butter, salt and boiling water. Mix well. Let cool to lukewarm. Combine yeast with 1/4 cup warm water. Let stand a few minutes to soften yeast. Add 2 cups unbleached flour to potato mixture; beat well. Stir in dissolved yeast. Mix in whole wheat flour until blended; beat well. Gradually stir in remaining 1 to 1 1/2 cups unbleached flour until mixture forms a stiff dough.

    Turn dough onto floured surface. Knead 5 to 7 minutes, adding additional flour as necessary. Place dough in greased 2 1/2 quart pan, turning dough to grease top; cover loosely with plastic wrap. When doubled in size, punch down. Knead a few times; divide dough in half. Shape each half into a loaf. Grease an 8x4-inch glass pan. Sprinkle with toasted wheat germ, coating bottom and sides of pan. Place dough in dish, smooth side up. Grease tops of loaves. Cover loosely with plastic wrap. Place both loaves in microwave. Microwave on 10% power for 6 to 8 minutes. Let stand 15 to 25 minutes. Remove plastic wrap. Cover each loaf with paper towel. Microwave on 50% power one loaf at a time 9 to 10 minutes. Cool 5 minutes. Turn out of dish. Repeat with remaining loaf. Cool completely.

Preparation time: 2 1/2 hours      Yield: 2 loaves
    Hint: Dough can be baked, uncovered, at 375 degrees for 35 to 40 minutes after it has been microwaved on 10% power for 6 to 8 minutes.

Diana Ruden
Marcus, Iowa

# MOIST WHOLE WHEAT BREAD

2 c. milk
1/2 c. honey
1/2 c. oil
7 c. whole wheat flour, sifted
  (flour is used in 2 separate
  steps)

1 egg, room temperature
1/2 c. warm water
1 Tbsp. honey
2 pkg. dry yeast
1 Tbsp. salt

Heat milk until hot, but do not scald. Add 1/2 cup honey and oil to milk; blend. Add to 4 cups flour. When mixed well, add egg and mix thoroughly again. Let this mixture stand at least one hour for better bread texture. This lets the liquid soften the bran. (I make this up at night in a large container, cover and let stand all night. I do not refrigerate, but if you do, be sure to let dough return to room temperature before adding remaining ingredients.) When ready to proceed, mix 1/2 cup warm water with 1 tablespoon honey; then add 2 packages yeast. Stir to dissolve. Let this mixture rise until doubled to activate yeast. Add to previously mixed dough. Stir together 1 tablespoon salt and remaining 3 cups flour; add to dough.

Knead right in the container in which dough was mixed, being sure it is large enough for kneading without spilling flour and will hold dough after it has doubled. Knead until dough pulls off bottom of container and blisters form on outside. (This mixture will be workable, but a lot stickier than dough made with white flour.) Kneading will take from 3-5 minutes if you are working hard. You cannot overknead, so if in doubt, keep kneading. Cover; let rise until doubled; knead down. Cover and let rise again until doubled. Knead down again and let rest for 10 minutes. On a lightly greased surface, form into loaves, making sure all bubbles have been worked out. Put into greased bread pans and let rise to top of pans. Bake for 30 minutes at 350 degrees. Bread is done if bottom of loaf is a medium brown color when you turn it upside down. The tops of loaves brown quickly, so after 15-20 minutes, cover tops with aluminum foil for remainder of baking time. Stays fresh and moist if kept frozen, and slices better. Makes 3 loaves, 9x5 inches or 8x4 inches. Triple recipe for 9-10 loaves.

Preparation time: overnight +     Yield: 3 loaves
          4 hours

Donna M. Harrison
Millington, Tennessee

## WHEAT-OAT BREAD

3 pkg. yeast
4 c. warm water
1/2 c. honey
1 Tbsp. salt
1/4 c. oil

1 1/2 c. oats
1/2 c. wheat germ
1 c. soy grits
6 c. whole wheat flour

Dissolve yeast, warm water, and honey. Let stand 10 minutes in warm place until foamy. Add salt, and oil, then oats, wheat germ, soy grits, and flour. Mix and knead well until elastic. Place in 2 large loaf pans. Bake 15 minutes at 275 degrees, then bake 30-40 minutes more at 350 degrees. No need to let rise before baking.

Preparation time: 1 hour          Yield: 2 loaves

Janet Hillstrand
Harlan, Iowa

## WHOLE WHEAT FRENCH BREAD

1 pkg. yeast
1 1/4 c. warm water (105-115 degrees)
1 1/2 tsp. salt
1 Tbsp. butter or margarine

2 c. whole wheat flour
1 1/2 - 2 c. unbleached flour
Corn meal
Cold water

Dissolve yeast in warm water; let stand 5 minutes. Stir in salt, butter and 2 cups whole wheat flour. Beat until smooth (with mixer or by hand). Stir in unbleached flour, enough to make dough easy to handle. Turn dough onto lightly floured surface; knead about 5 minutes. Place in greased bowl, turn. Cover with warm damp cloth, place in warm place to rise until double (2 hours). Punch dough down, let rise until double (1 hour). Punch dough down again, let rest (covered) 15 minutes.

Sprinkle corn meal on lightly greased cookie sheet. Shape dough into 15x10 inch rectangle; roll up and seal edge. Place on baking sheet; brush with cold water. Make 1/4 inch slashes across loaf, 2 inches apart. Let rise uncovered 1 1/2 hours. Brush with cold water.

Heat oven to 375 degrees. Bake 45 minutes.

Preparation time: approximately          Yield: 1 loaf
                  6 1/2 hours

Cindy Mahan
Spokane, Washington

## EASY FRENCH BREAD—THE FOOD PROCESSOR WAY

4 c. flour (1/2 whole wheat,       1 1/2 Tbsp. yeast (1 1/2 pkg.)
  1/2 unbleached)                      2 tsp. salt
                                    1 Tbsp. honey
                                    1 1/2 c. warm water

Dump everything in food processor except water. Pour water down feed tube as you turn machine on. Let all ingredients knead together, approximately 15 seconds. Put dough in bowl (greased is best) and let rise about an hour. Punch down and mold into desired shape. Let rise again, about 30 minutes. Bake at 375-400 degrees for 15-20 minutes.

Preparation time: 1 hour 45 minutes  Yield: 1 large loaf, 2 small loaves,
                                               or 6-8 hamburger sized buns

Diane McLean
Knoxville, Tennessee


## AUNT LOU'S FANCY BRAIDED BREAD

4 1/2 c. unbleached flour         2 1/4 c. very warm water
1/4 c. honey                      1 1/4 c. whole wheat flour
1 Tbsp. salt                      1 1/4 c. rye flour
1/4 c. melted margarine        1 Tbsp. carob powder
2 pkg. yeast                     Caraway seeds

Combine 2 1/4 cups unbleached flour, honey, salt, yeast, margarine, and water. Beat for two minutes at medium speed. Add one more cup of unbleached flour and beat on high for three minutes. Divide batter into three bowls.

Make whole wheat dough by beating in whole wheat flour into 1/3 of the batter. Make rye dough by adding carob powder and rye flour to 1/3 of batter. Make white dough by beating 1 1/4 cups unbleached flour into remaining batter.

Knead each dough until smooth and elastic, about 4 minutes. Cover. Let rise in warm place until doubled, about 1 hour. Punch down. On floured board, divide each dough in half. Roll each piece into a 15-inch rope. On a greased baking sheet, braid together a white, whole wheat, and rye rope. Pinch ends to seal. Repeat with remaining dough. Cover, let rise until doubled, about 1 hour. Sprinkle with caraway seeds.

Bake at 350 degrees for 35-40 minutes.

Preparation time: 3 hours           Yield: two loaves

Lou Sutton
Harrison, Arkansas

# COOL RISE SWEET DOUGH

5-6 c. unbleached flour
2 pkg. dry yeast
1 1/2 tsp. salt
1/2 c. softened butter or margarine

1/3 c. honey
1 1/2 c. hot tap water
2 eggs, room temperature

Combine 2 cups flour, undissolved yeast and salt in large bowl. Stir well to blend. Add butter and honey, then add hot tap water all at once. Beat with electric mixer at medium speed for 2 minutes or in food processor until mixed well. Add eggs and 1 cup flour. Beat at high speed until thick and elastic. Gradually stir in enough remaining flour to make soft dough (will leave sides of bowl). Knead dough until smooth, 5-10 minutes by hand or use food processor. Cover with plastic wrap, then a towel. Let rest for 20 minutes or longer. Punch down, divide and shape as desired. Place on greased sheets or pans. Cover loosely with plastic wrap. Refrigerate 2-24 hours. When ready to bake, remove from refrigerator, let rise and bake at 375 degrees for 20 minutes or until golden brown.

Preparation time: 40 minutes +
   2-24 hours refrigeration +
   1 1/2 hours rising and baking

Yield: 24 dinner rolls

   Hint: These may be frozen after shaping. Allow plenty of time for thawing and rising.

Karen Shrum
Harrison, Arkansas

## REFRIGERATOR ROLLS

1 3/4 c. milk
1/2 c. oil
1/2 c. honey
1 pkg. dry yeast
1/4 c. very warm water

6 c. unbleached flour
1/2 tsp. soda
1/2 tsp. baking powder
1 Tbsp. salt

Scald first 3 ingredients; cool to lukewarm. Dissolve yeast in very warm water; add to milk mixture. In large bowl, mix well: 3 cups flour with the milk-yeast mixture. Let rise in warm place, covered, for 2 hours or until double. Sift soda, baking powder and salt with 1 cup of flour. Add remaining flour, kneading well until dough is like an elastic ball. Roll out for pocketbook rolls. Let rise, covered, until double in warm place; then bake at 400 degrees for 10 minutes or until browned. Or, the dough, covered, will keep ten days in the refrigerator.

Preparation time: 4 hours (if baking
          the same day)

Yield: 30-35 rolls

   Hint: For cold dough, put rolls out in the A.M. on counter top and let rise all day. Perfect for supper baking, and easy on the working girl.

Mrs. Bradford White
Memphis, Tennessee

# RAISIN COFFEE CAKE

| | |
|---|---|
| 1/8 c. wheat germ | 1/2 c. water |
| 1/8 c. soy flour | 1 c. butter |
| 5 - 5 1/4 c. unbleached flour | 2 eggs, room temperature |
| 1/4 c. honey | 2 c. chopped walnuts |
| 1 tsp. salt | 2/3 c. raisins |
| 1 tsp. grated lemon peel | 3 Tbsp. date sugar |
| 2 Tbsp. yeast | 3 Tbsp. honey |
| 1 c. milk | 1 Tbsp. butter |

In a large bowl thoroughly mix wheat germ, soy flour, 2 cups flour, honey, salt, lemon peel, and yeast. Combine milk, water and butter in a saucepan. Heat over low heat until liquids are very warm, but butter does not need to melt. Gradually add to dry ingredients and beat 2 minutes at medium speed of mixer. Add eggs and 1/2 cup flour. Beat at high speed 2 minutes. Stir in enough additional flour to make a stiff dough. Cover bowl with plastic wrap, then a towel. Set aside for 20 minutes.

Combine walnuts, raisins and date sugar. Turn dough out onto heavily floured board. Divide dough in half. Roll each half into a 14x10-inch rectangle. Spread with raisin filling. Roll up from long side as for jelly roll to form a roll 14 inches long. Pinch seam to seal. Place on a greased baking sheet. Cut diagonal slits about 1 inch apart in roll, starting from top surface of roll and cutting about 2/3 of the way through. Pull cut pieces out alternately right and left. Cover loosely with wax paper brushed with oil, then top with plastic wrap.

Refrigerate 2-24 hours. When ready to bake, remove from refrigerator. Uncover dough carefully. Let stand at room temperature for 10 minutes. Bake at 375 degrees for 25-30 minutes or until done. Remove from baking sheets and cool. Warm 3 tablespoons honey and 1 tablespoon butter. Spread on top of the coffee cakes.

Preparation time: 1 hour +
            rising time

Yield: 14-16 servings

Tina Riley
Mt. Carmel, Illinois


# PIZZA CRUST

| | |
|---|---|
| 1 pkg. yeast (1 Tbsp. active dry yeast) | 1/2 tsp. honey |
| 1 c. warm water | 3 c. unbleached white or whole wheat flour (use a combination |
| 1 Tbsp. oil | that you like) |

Combine ingredients and knead; let rise 10 minutes. Roll out and spread in 2-3 pans. Cover with your choice of sauce and toppings. Bake at 500 degrees until done.

Preparation time: 40 minutes        Yield: 2-3 crusts

Jeralyn Volkert
Marcus, Iowa

# HONEY HAMBURGER BUNS

8 c. unbleached flour
  (or 1/2 whole wheat)
2 pkg. active dry yeast
2 c. warm water

3/4 c. oil
1/4 - 1/2 c. honey
1 Tbsp. salt
3 eggs, room temperature

In large bowl, combine 4 cups flour and yeast. Combine water, oil, honey, and salt; add to dry mixture in bowl. Add eggs. Beat at low speed for 1/2 minute, then at high speed for 3 minutes. By hand, stir in enough remaining flour to make a soft dough. Cover, let rise until double, 1 hour. Punch down, divide dough in 3 portions; cover and let rise 5 minutes. Divide each portion of dough into 8 balls and shape into buns. Place on greased baking sheet and press to 3 1/2 inch circle. Let rise until double, about 30 minutes. Bake at 375 degrees for 10 minutes. Can be frozen.

Preparation time: 2 1/2 hours     Yield: 24 buns

Sue Riddle
Republic, Missouri


# HAMBURGER BUNS

1 pkg. active dry yeast
1 c. warm water
1 Tbsp. honey
1 tsp. salt

1 egg
2 Tbsp. butter (or 1 Tbsp.
  butter and 1/2 Tbsp. oil)
2 3/4 c. flour (whole wheat or
  unbleached or combination
  to taste)

Dissolve yeast in warm water in large mixing bowl. Add honey, salt, egg, butter (or oil) and 1 cup flour. Beat until smooth. Add the remaining flour and stir until smooth. Scrape batter from side of bowl, then cover and let rise in warm place until doubled—approximately 30-40 minutes. Stir batter down. Turn onto floured surface and roll out about 1/4 inch thick. Cut into 12 equal parts. (I use a coffee mug to cut shapes.) Roll shapes into balls and place on cookie sheet. (Cookie sheet should be lightly greased and balls should be approximately 1 inch apart.) Let rise, covered, until doubled approximately 30 minutes.

Heat oven to 400 degrees and bake about 15 minutes. Cut as desired in halves.

Preparation time: 1 1/2 hours     Yield: 12 buns

Carolyn Hoelscher
Ballwin, Missouri

SALADS

# CALIFORNIA CHEF'S SALAD

6 c. bite-size salad greens
2 cans (7 oz.) white tuna, drained
1 c. Monterey Jack or Cheddar
  cheese

8 slices bacon, crumbled
1/2 c. celery
1 avocado
4 slices tomato

Mix all except avocado and tomato which are used for garnish.

Preparation time: 10-15 minutes     Yield: 4 large servings

Janet Griffin
Grand Junction, Colorado

# RAW BEET AND CARROT SALAD

1 medium fresh beet, grated
1 large carrot, grated
1/2 c. raisins

1/2 c. unsweetened coconut
2 Tbsp. homemade mayonnaise

Toss ingredients gently, chill, and serve.

Preparation time: 10 minutes     Yield: 3-4 servings
    Hint: This is delicious, easy and very colorful.

Betty Vanderschaaf
Orange City, Iowa

# LENTIL SALAD

1 c. dry lentils
2 Tbsp. oil
1 c. bulgur wheat
1/2 c. soy grits
1 large onion, chopped
2 tsp. salt
2 c. plain yogurt

4 Tbsp. mayonnaise
2 tsp. garlic powder
2 tsp. mustard
4 tsp. lemon juice
Scallions
Red onions

Cook lentils and drain. Put oil in heavy skillet. Over medium heat toast grains. Stir constantly for 5-10 minutes. Add 2 cups hot water, onion and salt. Cover and cook over low heat for 10 minutes until light and fluffy. Combine yogurt, mayonnaise, garlic powder, mustard and lemon juice; mix thoroughly with wire wisk and add to lentils. Add scallions and red onions as desired.

Preparation time: 1 hour     Yield: 6-8 servings

Janet Hillstrand
Harlan, Iowa

# FRESH SPINACH SALAD

1 lb. spinach, fresh, cut
  with scissors
4-5 strips bacon, fried
  and crumbled
Handful of bean sprouts

2-3 hard boiled eggs, chopped
1/2 - 1 c. croutons (from whole
  wheat bread), cubed and
  browned in butter

Prepare and combine spinach, bacon, bean sprouts and eggs. Add croutons and dressing just before serving.

**Dressing:**

1 c. oil
1/2 c. honey
1/2 c. vinegar
1 (8 oz.) can tomato sauce

1 Tbsp. Worcestershire sauce
1 medium onion, chopped
1/2 tsp. salt

Blend together in blender and refrigerate for 1 hour.

Preparation time: 20 minutes     Yield: 4-6 servings

Mrs. George Dixon
Milford, Illinois

# BECKY'S SPINACH SALAD

1/4 lb. fresh spinach
1/2 c. green onions, with
  tops, sliced fine
1/4 c. oil
2 Tbsp. red wine vinegar
1 Tbsp. lemon juice
1/2 tsp. fructose

1/2 tsp. salt
Dash of pepper
6 mushrooms, sliced fine
4 slices crisp bacon,
  crumbled
2 hard boiled eggs, chopped

Wash and dry spinach, tear into bite-size pieces and remove stems. Combine onions, oil, vinegar, lemon juice, fructose, salt, pepper and mushrooms. Chill thoroughly or heat on low. Add to spinach just before serving; top with bacon and chopped eggs. Toss.

Preparation time: 15 minutes     Yield: 6 servings

Becky Bull
Harrison, Arkansas

# SPINACH SALAD

1 head iceberg lettuce
1 lb. fresh spinach
1 pkg. frozen green peas,
  uncooked
8-12 slices bacon, cooked
  and crumbled

6 chopped boiled eggs
2 c. homemade mayonnaise
8 oz. sour cream
2 pkg. Hidden Valley Ranch™
  dressing

Layer first 5 ingredients in order given. Mix mayonnaise, sour cream, and Hidden Valley dressing. Spread over layered mixture. Refrigerate overnight. Stir before serving.

Preparation time: 20-25 minutes +          Yield: 10-12 servings
                  overnight refrigeration

Karen Shrum
Harrison, Arkansas


# ORANGE SPINACH SALAD

1 lb. fresh spinach, washed
  and drained
1 large orange, sectioned
  (or 2 small)
1 small red onion, sliced thin
1/4 c. oil

2 Tbsp. tarragon wine vinegar
1 Tbsp. honey
1/2 tsp. dry mustard
1/2 tsp. salt
1 clove garlic, cut in half
Dash of pepper

Tear spinach in bite size pieces. Place in salad bowl with oranges and onion. Stir together oil, vinegar, honey, mustard, salt, garlic and pepper. At serving time, remove garlic, stir dressing and pour over salad.

Preparation time: 20 minutes          Yield: 6-8 servings
    Hint: You may want to reduce the onion to half. Make the dressing in advance if garlic flavor is desired, or substitute a dash of garlic powder if there is no time.

Debi Thullen
Berkley, Michigan

# CAULIFLOWER SALAD

4 c. thinly sliced raw
  cauliflower
1 c. coarsely chopped
  pitted ripe olives

2/3 c. coarsely chopped
  green pepper
1/2 c. coarsely chopped pimento
1/2 c. chopped onion

### Dressing:

1/2 c. olive oil
3 Tbsp. lemon juice
3 Tbsp. wine vinegar

2 tsp. salt
1/2 tsp. fructose
1/4 tsp. pepper

Combine all vegetables. Combine dressing ingredients. Mix together and chill 4 hours or overnight. Line bowl with salad greens and spoon into center.

Preparation time: 20-30 minutes +
                4 hours chilling time

Yield: 6-8 servings

Mary G. Bratt
Waldo, Ohio


# TOMATO ASPIC (Salt Free)

2 c. unsalted tomato juice
1 bay leaf
4 whole cloves
1 slice onion

6 peppercorns
1 Tbsp. unflavored gelatin
1 Tbsp. lemon juice
1 Tbsp. tarragon vinegar

Measure 1 1/2 cups tomato juice in saucepan; add bay leaf, cloves, onion and peppercorns. Bring to a boil and simmer for 10 minutes; strain. Soften gelatin in remaining 1/2 cup tomato juice and dissolve in hot juice. Add lemon juice. Pour into mold and chill until firm.

Preparation time: 10 minutes +
              gelling time

Yield: 4 servings

Mrs. E.C. Shackleford
Hollandale, Mississippi

# CREAMY POTATO SALAD

7 to 8 medium potatoes
1/4 c. oil
1/4 c. cider vinegar
1 Tbsp. salt
1/2 tsp. pepper
1 c. finely chopped onion

1 c. diced green pepper
1 c. celery, sliced diagonally
1/2 c. homemade mayonnaise
1/2 c. sour cream
Leaf lettuce
Tomato wedges

Cook potatoes in boiling salted water to cover in a large saucepan until tender, about 30 minutes. Drain, peel, and cut in large cubes into a large bowl. Add oil, vinegar, salt, pepper, and onion. Toss just until potatoes are moistened. Cover; refrigerate 2 to 3 hours, until marinade is absorbed. Add green pepper and celery. Combine mayonnaise and sour cream; toss gently to coat all ingredients. Chill until serving time. To serve, line salad bowl with lettuce, mound potato salad in center, and arrange tomato wedges around edge.

Preparation time: 4 hours,
    counting marinade time

Yield: 12 servings

Judy Beemer
Sharon Spring, Kansas


# FRUIT-NUT SLAW

4 c. finely shredded cabbage
1/2 c. finely diced celery
1 c. chopped, unpeeled apples

1/2 c. grated carrots
1/4 c. raisins
1/2 c. chopped walnuts

   Dressing:

1/3 c. homemade mayonnaise
1/3 c. plain yogurt
1 Tbsp. lemon juice
1 tsp. honey

1/4 tsp. salt
1/4 tsp. ginger
1/4 tsp. curry powder

Combine all ingredients except walnuts. Mix dressing and pour over salad immediately. Stir in walnuts just before serving.

Preparation time: 15 minutes

Yield: 8-10 servings

Terry L. Praznik
Prairie Village, Kansas

## HONEY SLAW

4 c. chopped cabbage
1/2 c. cream

1/4 c. honey
2 Tbsp. apple cider vinegar

Combine cream, honey and vinegar. Pour over cabbage and mix well.

Preparation time: 15 minutes          Yield: 6 servings
    Hint: For extra interest add either 1/4 cup mung or alfalfa sprouts or 1 cup chopped fruit.

Mrs. Lloyd Utke
Billings, Montana


## HONEY FRUIT SALAD

1 (15 1/4 oz.) can unsweetened
  pineapple chunks, undrained
2 medium oranges, peeled
  and sectioned
1 medium apple, peeled and
  sliced

1 banana, peeled and sliced
1/2 c. chopped pecans
1/2 c. orange juice
1 Tbsp. lemon juice
1/4 c. honey

Combine first five ingredients in large bowl. Combine orange juice, lemon juice and honey in a small bowl and mix well. Pour over fruit, tossing gently. Chill thoroughly.

Preparation time: 15 minutes          Yield: 4-6 servings

Genevieve Russell
Dallas, Texas


## BANANA NUT SALAD

2 bananas
1/4 c. homemade mayonnaise
1 Tbsp. honey

1 Tbsp. natural style peanut
  butter
1/4 c. chopped nuts

Cut bananas in halves crosswise, then lengthwise. Combine mayonnaise, peanut butter and honey; spoon over bananas. Sprinkle nuts on top of bananas.

Preparation time: 10 minutes          Yield: 4 servings

Debi Thullen
Berkley, Michigan

# ORANGE ALMOND SALAD

| | |
|---|---|
| 1/4 c. oil | 3 medium oranges, peeled and |
| 2 Tbsp. honey | sliced, crosswise and halved |
| 2 Tbsp. vinegar (wine) | 1/2 c. thinly sliced celery |
| 1/4 tsp. salt | 2 Tbsp. sliced green onions |
| 1/8 tsp. almond extract | 1/3 c. toasted slivered almonds |
| 6 c. mixed salad greens | |

Mix dressing together first by combining the first 5 ingredients in a jar. Cover and shake well; chill. Combine oranges, vegetables and almonds. Pour dressing over and toss gently to coat. Serve at once.

Preparation time: 15 minutes     Yield: 6-8 servings

Diane McLean
Knoxville, Tennessee

# FRUIT YOGURT SALAD

| | |
|---|---|
| 1 c. plain yogurt | 3 ripe bananas, sliced |
| 1/2 c. crushed, drained | Chopped nuts |
| pineapple (fresh or canned | 1/2 c. crushed fresh berries |
| in own juice) | (strawberries or raspberries) |
| 1 Tbsp. honey | |

Mix together yogurt, pineapple, honey and bananas. Sprinkle with nuts and crushed berries. Chill for 2 hours before serving.

Preparation time: 15 minutes +     Yield: 4 servings
                2 hours

Ruth Ann Peters
Harrison, Arkansas

# FRUIT SALAD

| | |
|---|---|
| 1 large can sliced pineapple | 1/2 c. unsweetened coconut |
| 2 bananas | 1/2 c. chopped nuts |
| 1 can unsweetened Mandarin | 2 Tbsp. honey |
| oranges (or 1 1/2 c. fresh | 2 beaten eggs |
| orange sections) | 2 Tbsp. cornstarch |

Drain pineapple juice into saucepan. In another bowl, cut pineapple slices into chunks, slice bananas; add orange sections, coconut and nuts. Add honey, eggs, and cornstarch to pineapple juice. Cook together until thick. Pour over fruit mixture. Chill.

Preparation time: 15 minutes +     Yield: 4-6 servings
                chilling time

Janet Redding
Pasadena, California

## PINEAPPLE-ORANGE MOLD

1 envelope unflavored gelatin
1 c. pure orange juice
2 Tbsp. fructose
1/4 - 1/2 tsp. salt
1 Tbsp. lemon juice

1/2 c. sliced carrots
1 c. crushed pineapple with
its own juice
1/4 tsp. almond extract

Sprinkle gelatin over 1/2 cup orange juice in blender to soften. Bring remaining orange juice to a simmer, add to blender and run on low speed 1 minute, then add fructose, salt, and lemon juice, plus sliced carrots. Blend at medium speed 1 minute or until smooth. Pour mixture in bowl. Add pineapple with its own juice and almond extract. Mix well, pour into 3-cup mold and refrigerate.

Preparation time: 20 minutes plus
molding time

Yield: 4 servings

Rita Hartel
Murray, Nebraska

## FROZEN PINEAPPLE SALAD

1 (3 oz.) pkg. cream cheese,
softened
1 (8 oz.) carton yogurt, (I use
honey sweetened yogurt to
add color)

1 (8 1/2 oz.) can unsweetened
crushed pineapple, drained
Chopped nuts

Blend cream cheese and yogurt. Stir in crushed pineapple. Spoon into paper baking cups in muffin pan. Cover and freeze until firm. Remove paper cups from salads. Arrange on lettuce leaves and top with nuts. Can also stir nuts into mixture or sprinkle on top before freezing.

Preparation time: 10 minutes +
freezing time

Yield: 6-8 servings

Jeralyn Volkert
Marcus, Iowa

# OLIVE-EGG-RICE SALAD

3 c. cooked brown rice
1 c. chopped grated onion
1 c. sliced ripe olives
2 Tbsp. diced pimento
2 Tbsp. chopped parsley

1/2 c. homemade mayonnaise
1/4 c. creamy French dressing
1 Tbsp. lemon juice
3 grated hard-cooked eggs
Tomatoes

Combine rice, onion, olives, pimento, and parsley; season to taste with salt. Blend mayonnaise, French dressing and lemon juice. Stir in eggs and spoon the dressing over the rice mixture. Garnish with tomato wedges.

Preparation time: 15 minutes          Yield: 6 servings

Mrs. Charles F. Morgan
Knoxville, Tennessee


**Editor's note: For Creamy French Dressing, use this recipe:**

1/3 c. honey
1/3 c. apple cider vinegar
3 Tbsp. powdered milk
1 Tbsp. lemon juice
1 tsp. dry mustard

1 tsp. paprika
1 tsp. celery seed
1 tsp. minced onion
1/4 tsp. salt
1 c. oil

Blend all ingredients in a blender or food processor except the oil; add it in a steady stream and mix thoroughly for 1-2 minutes.

Preparation time: 5 minutes          Yield: 2 cups


# CURRY CHICKEN SALAD

1 chicken, cooked and deboned
2 stalks celery
1 apple (with or without
   peeling)

2 Tbsp. homemade mayonnaise
   with 2 Tbsp. lemon juice and
   1 Tbsp. curry powder
1/4 c. chopped pecans

Mix and serve as sandwich or on greens as a salad.

Preparation time: 15 minutes          Yield: 6-8 servings

Jan Berryhill
Richmond, Virginia

## CHICKEN AND RICE SALAD

1 1/2 c. cubed cooked chicken
1 c. long grain brown rice
  (cooked in 2 c. boiling
  water for 15 minutes)

3/4 c. cubed Cheddar cheese (mild)
1/4 c. chopped onions
3 Tbsp. lemon juice
Salt and pepper to taste

Combine chicken, rice, onions, lemon juice and seasonings. Add cheese last. Toss together lightly and serve immediately. This salad has a very delicate taste.

Preparation time: 30 minutes     Yield: 4 servings

Judy Harned
Coyle, Oklahoma


## CHICKEN-CARROT SALAD

5 grated carrots
1 1/2 c. chopped celery

2 Tbsp. grated onion
2 c. cooked chicken, chopped
1/2 c. homemade mayonnaise
1/2 c. milk

Mix vegetables and chicken. Before serving, add 1/2 cup homemade mayonnaise thinned with 1/2 cup milk.

Preparation time: 15 minutes     Yield: Serves 6

Mrs. Charles F. Morgan
Knoxville, Tennessee


## HOT CHINESE CHICKEN SALAD

8 chicken thighs, skinned,
  boned and cut in 1 inch cubes
1/4 c. cornstarch
1/4 c. oil
1 c. coarsely chopped onion
1 c. slant-sliced celery

1 large ripe tomato, cut in
  chunks
1 (4 oz.) can mushrooms, sliced
1/4 c. soy sauce or tamari
1/8 tsp. garlic powder
2 c. finely shredded lettuce

Coat chicken in cornstarch and cook in oil over medium temperature until brown. Add remaining ingredients except lettuce and stir. Cover and simmer 5 minutes. To serve, place lettuce in bowl and add chicken mixture. Serve hot over rice.

Preparation time: 1 1/2 hours     Yield: 4 generous servings

Claudia Tanner
Eaton Rapids, Michigan

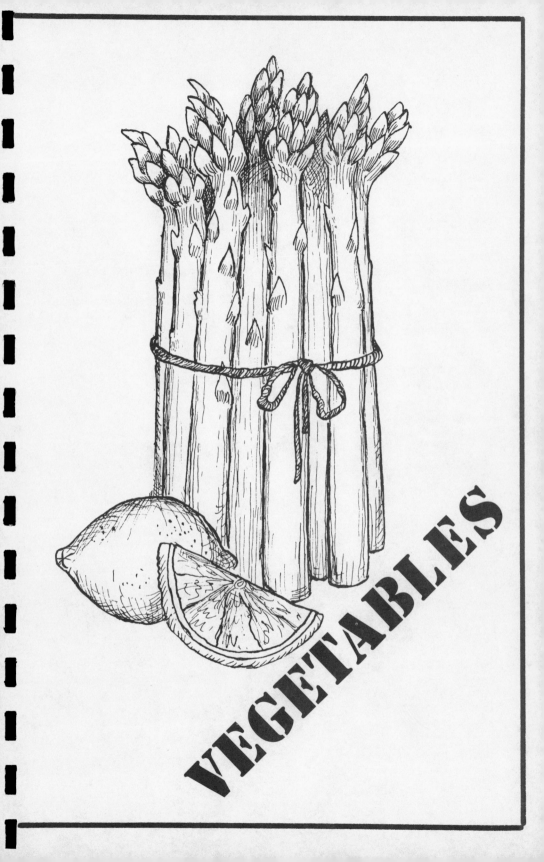

VEGETABLES

## CONCOMBERS PLACES

3 medium cucumbers (not
  bitter!)
3 Tbsp. butter

1 c. sour cream
1 egg yolk
Salt and pepper

Preheat oven to 375 degrees. Peel whole cucumbers. Cut in quarters, lengthwise. Remove seeds. Cube cucumbers. Pour in buttered casserole dish and garnish with butter. Bake for 30 minutes. Check; if done, add the sour cream mixed with the yolk. Cook 3 minutes longer. **Do not** let boil after adding the sour cream.

Preparation time: 1 hour          Yield: 6 servings

Lise Stevens
Gainesville, Missouri

## DEVILED TOMATOES

6 medium tomatoes
1/2 tsp. seasoned salt
1/4 tsp. black pepper
2 Tbsp. butter or margarine

2 tsp. Worcestershire sauce
  (optional)
1/8 tsp. Tabasco sauce
1/2 tsp. Dijon type mustard
1/2 c. dry bread crumbs

Cut tomatoes in halves and place in shallow baking dish, cut side up. Sprinkle lightly with salt and pepper. Melt butter, add seasonings. Stir in bread crumbs. Spoon on top of tomatoes. Bake 15 minutes at 350 degrees or until crumbs are brown.

Preparation time: 30 minutes          Yield: 6 servings

Mrs. Monroe Dunn
Belzoni, Mississippi

## RUSSIAN CABBAGE

3 Tbsp. butter
3 Tbsp. onion, chopped
3 Tbsp. chopped green pepper
2 c. tomatoes, chopped
1 tsp. salt
1/4 tsp. pepper

3 c. cooked shredded cabbage
1/2 c. buttered whole wheat
  bread crumbs
1/2 c. grated Cheddar cheese

Saute onion and green pepper in butter until slightly brown. Add tomatoes, salt and pepper. Put half of cabbage in greased casserole. Alternate layers with tomato mixture. Sprinkle bread crumbs and cheese on top. Bake at 350 degrees for 20 minutes.

Preparation time: 30 minutes          Yield: 4-6 servings

Mrs. George Dixon
Milford, Illinois

## CREAMY CABBAGE

6 c. shredded cabbage
1/3 c. water
1/8 tsp. salt
1/4 c. chopped onion (optional)
3 oz. cream cheese, cubed

1/2 tsp. celery seed
2 Tbsp. butter or margarine
Paprika
1 tsp. salt

Cook or steam cabbage in water with salt and onion for about 7 minutes. Drain and add remaining ingredients, toss, and serve.

Preparation time: 20 minutes        Yield: Serves 6

Mrs. James Anderson
Rock Falls, Illinois

## MOM'S CRAZY CABBAGE

1 1/2 lb. ground beef
1 large onion, chopped
1 head of cabbage

1 large can tomatoes
3 strips of bacon
Salt and pepper

Brown ground beef and chopped onion in skillet. Set aside. Chop cabbage and place half in bottom of 13x9 inch baking dish. Sprinkle meat over cabbage and then top with remaining cabbage. Pour the can of tomatoes over meat and cabbage mixture. Top with bacon, salt and pepper. Cover dish with foil and bake for 3 hours in 325-350 degree oven.

Preparation time: 3 1/4 hours        Yield: 6 servings

Becky Bull
Harrison, Arkansas

## QUICK CABBAGE

1 medium head cabbage

1/4 c. butter or margarine
Tabasco sauce

Shred the cabbage coarsely, drop in 1 cup of boiling, salted water with a dash of Tabasco added. Cover and cook 10-15 minutes, drain. Pour 1/4 cup melted butter or margarine over the cabbage and toss well. Serve immediately.

Preparation time: 25 minutes        Yield: 6 servings
   Hint: Cabbage will retain more nutrients if steamed rather than boiled.

Mrs. Monroe Dunn
Belzoni, Mississippi

# CHEESY CELERY

| | |
|---|---|
| 1 stalk celery, cut in 1/2 inch pieces | 1 c. sharp Cheddar cheese, grated |
| 3 Tbsp. butter | Salt to taste |
| 3 Tbsp. unbleached flour | Buttered bread crumbs |
| 3/4 c. evaporated milk | |

Cook celery in boiling, salted water 10-15 minutes. Drain and set aside. Melt 3 tablespoons butter in saucepan, blend in flour and milk and stir until thickened. Add cheese, celery and salt. Place in buttered casserole, top with crumbs and bake 15-20 minutes at 375 degrees.

Preparation time: 40 minutes          Yield: 4 servings

Judy Britton
Richmond, Virginia


# CREAMED SPINACH

| | |
|---|---|
| 1 (10 oz.) pkg. frozen spinach (cooked and well drained) | 1/4 c. butter |
| 3 oz. cream cheese | Salt to taste |
| | Artichoke hearts (optional) |
| | Bread crumbs (optional) |

Cook spinach and drain thoroughly. Melt cream cheese and butter together, then add to spinach; salt to taste. May be served like this or put artichoke hearts in the bottom of a casserole dish; add spinach. Top with bread crumbs and bake at 350 degrees until bubbly.

Preparation time: 20-30 minutes          Yield: 4 servings
    Hint: Steam vegetables when possible to retain vitamin content.

Betsy Branstetter
Kansas City, Missouri


# BROCCOLI CASSEROLE

| | |
|---|---|
| 1 (10 oz.) pkg. frozen (or fresh) broccoli spears | 1 can (or fresh cooked) mushrooms |
| 1 can cream of celery soup (undiluted) | Grated Cheddar cheese |
| | Whole wheat bread crumbs, buttered, or wheat germ |

Alternate layers of broccoli, mushrooms, cream of celery soup and cheese. (Save 2 tablespoons cheese for topping). Make 2 layers, then top with bread crumbs and cheese. Bake, uncovered, at 350 degrees until bubbly and topping is golden brown.

Preparation time: 40 minutes          Yield: 6 servings

Shirley Nickels
Vancouver, Washington

## BEAN CASSEROLE

1 (10 oz.) pkg. frozen French
   style green beans
1 (10 oz.) pkg. lima beans

1 (10 oz.) pkg. frozen green
   peas

Steam above vegetables until crisp-tender. Meanwhile prepare the sauce below.

**Sauce:**

1 1/2 c. homemade mayonnaise
1 medium onion, finely chopped
1 Tbsp. brown mustard

3 boiled eggs, finely chopped
3 Tbsp. oil
Dash Tabasco sauce or cayenne

Mix all ingredients together. Place vegetables in serving bowl. Add salt and pepper to taste. Mix. Pour the sauce over vegetables. Stir and serve.

Preparation time: 15-20 minutes     Yield: 8-10 servings
Hint: For a smaller amount leave out one of the vegetables. Use 1 cup mayonnaise, 2 eggs, and 2 tablespoons oil.

Sue Marie Brown
Nashville, Tennessee


## CARROT STRIPS

6-8 medium carrots
4 Tbsp. butter or margarine
1 Tbsp. chopped onion
1 Tbsp. chopped parsley
1 Tbsp. water

1 Tbsp. unbleached flour
1/2 c. milk
1/2 tsp. salt
Pepper to taste

Wash and scrape carrots. Cut lengthwise into 2-inch strips. Melt butter or margarine then add carrots, onion, parsley and water. Cover pan and simmer on low heat until tender (about 20 minutes), stirring frequently and adding 1-2 tablespoons water if necessary to prevent sticking. Add flour, mix well; then add milk and mix well. Season to taste with salt and pepper and let boil; serve immediately.

Preparation time: 30 minutes     Yield: 6 servings

Mrs. Monroe Dunn
Belzoni, Mississippi

# SWEET AND SOUR CARROTS

1 lb. carrots, sliced diagonally
1 medium green pepper
1 (8 oz.) can pineapple
   chunks, in own juice
1/4 c. fructose

1 Tbsp. cornstarch
1/2 tsp. salt
2 Tbsp. vinegar
2 tsp. soy sauce

In pan, cook carrots, covered, in small amount of lightly salted water until just tender, about 15 minutes. Add green pepper, cover and cook 3 minutes more; drain. Drain pineapple, reserving juice, add water to make 1/3 cup liquid. In saucepan, combine fructose, cornstarch and salt, stir in pineapple liquid, vinegar and soy sauce. Cook and stir until bubbly. Stir in vegetables and pineapple. Heat through.

Preparation time: 30-40 minutes    Yield: 6 servings

Mary G. Bratt
Waldo, Ohio


# BROCCOLI AND PEAS CASSEROLE

1 bunch fresh broccoli
   (or 10 oz. frozen)
1 (10 oz.) frozen peas
4 eggs, hard cooked and sliced
3 Tbsp. butter or margarine
2 Tbsp. unbleached flour
1 1/2 c. milk
1/4 tsp. pepper

1/4 tsp. salt
1 c. Cheddar cheese, grated
1/2 c. homemade mayonnaise
2 slices whole wheat bread
2 Tbsp. butter or margarine
1/4 c. Parmesan cheese, grated
1/4 c. roasted salted sunflower
   seeds

Cook broccoli and peas separately in small amount of water until barely tender and still bright green. In a buttered casserole dish, place broccoli spears with stems toward center. Add peas; top with sliced eggs. Melt butter in skillet and add flour, cooking to a paste. Add milk slowly while stirring constantly. Cook over low heat until thickened; add salt, pepper and 1/2 cup of cheese. Stir until cheese is melted and remove from heat. Add the mayonnaise and blend. Pour over vegetables and top with remaining 1/2 cup cheese. Make bread crumbs from bread, and mix with the 2 tablespoons melted butter. Put on top of casserole and sprinkle with the Parmesan cheese and sunflower seeds. Bake in a 375 degree oven for 20 minutes.

Preparation time: 45 minutes    Yield: 6 servings

Mrs. Carl F. Maples, Sr.
Knoxville, Tennessee

# BROCCOLI ITALIAN STYLE

1 bunch broccoli
4-5 Tbsp. olive oil
3 Tbsp. onion, minced
1 clove garlic, peeled and
  chopped

1/2 tsp. oregano
3/4 Tbsp. salt
3 Tbsp. water
Pinch of cayenne pepper

Wash broccoli. Peel lower stalks and split each lengthwise in quarters. Cut broccoli stalks and flowerets in coarse pieces. Heat oil in large pan, add onion and garlic. Cook slowly, covered, until tender. Add broccoli, water, salt, pepper and oregano. Cover tightly and cook slowly for about 15 minutes or until broccoli is tender.

Preparation time: 30 minutes          Yield: 6 servings

Mary G. Bratt
Waldo, Ohio

# ITALIAN EGGPLANT

1 small eggplant, unpeeled and
  cut into 1/2 inch slices
1/2 c. melted butter or
  margarine
1/2 c. homemade bread crumbs
1/4 tsp. salt

1/8 tsp. pepper
1/2 tsp. oregano, crushed (optional)
1 c. homemade spaghetti
  sauce
1 c. shredded Mozzarella or
  Provolone cheese

Dip eggplant in butter, then in mixture of crumbs, salt, pepper, oregano. Put on greased cookie sheet. Equally spoon sauce on each slice, then cheese. Bake at 425 degrees 10-15 minutes or until done.

Preparation time: 25 minutes          Yield: 4-6 servings

Mrs. William Umbel
Boardman, Ohio

# BAKED SUCCOTASH

1 1/2 c. cooked corn, fresh
  or frozen
1 1/2 c. cooked limas, fresh
  or frozen
2 oz. shredded Cheddar cheese

1 celery stalk, chopped
1/2 c. homemade mayonnaise
Salt and pepper to taste
1 c. whole wheat bread crumbs
Butter

Mix vegetables, cheese and mayonnaise. Put in a 1-quart greased casserole. Melt butter, then brown crumbs in it. Sprinkle over casserole. Bake at 350 degrees for 30 minutes.

Preparation time: 40 minutes          Yield: 6-8 servings

Mrs. George Dixon
Milford, Illinois

# EGGPLANT BAKE

1 unpeeled washed eggplant
1 large onion, sliced
1 large ripe tomato, peeled

Butter or margarine
Salt and pepper
Grated Parmesan cheese

Cut the ends off the eggplant and then slice into 1/2 inch thick slices. Slice the onion and tomato into 1/4 inch slices.

Butter or oil a large flat baking dish. Salt and pepper the eggplant slices on both sides and arrange in the bottom of the baking dish. Cover each slice with a slice of onion, then tomato. Salt and pepper lightly, then top each slice with a small pat of butter or margarine.

Cover tightly with foil and bake at 350 degrees for about 1 hour. Remove the foil and sprinkle each stack generously with Parmesan cheese. Cover and bake 10-15 minutes longer.

Preparation time: 1 1/2 hours          Yield: 6 servings

Mrs. Monroe Dunn
Belzoni, Mississippi

# HONEY BEETS

2 Tbsp. honey
1 Tbsp. cornstarch
1/4 c. water

1/4 c. cider vinegar
2 c. beets, cooked
1 Tbsp. butter

Mix honey and cornstarch. Add water and vinegar and boil 5 minutes. Add beets and cook slowly until they are heated; add butter and serve.

Preparation time: 15 minutes          Yield: 6 servings

Mrs. Lloyd Utke
Billings, Missouri

# ZUCCHINI-TOMATO CASSEROLE

1/2 onion, chopped
2 Tbsp. butter
3 c. sliced zucchini
3 tomatoes, peeled and chopped
Salt and pepper to taste

1/3 c. whole wheat bread crumbs
1/2 lb. Mozzarella cheese, grated
1/3 c. Parmesan cheese, grated
4 Tbsp. butter

Saute onion in butter. In buttered 1 1/2 quart casserole, layer 1/2 of zucchini, onion, tomatoes, spices, bread crumbs, Mozzarella cheese, Parmesan cheese and dots of butter. Repeat layers. Bake at 350 degrees, uncovered, for 45 minutes.

Preparation time: 1 hour          Yield: 4-6 servings

Beth Miller
Emporia, Kansas

## ZUCCHINI SOUFFLE

1/4 c. butter
1/4 c. unsifted unbleached
   flour
1 1/3 c. milk
1 tsp. salt
Dash pepper

1 Tbsp. grated onion
1 1/4 c. grated zucchini,
   squeezed of liquid
5 eggs, separated (room temp.)
1 tsp. cream of tartar
1/2 c. sharp Cheddar cheese

Melt butter in saucepan. Remove from heat. Blend in flour. Stir in milk slowly; cook over low heat, stirring until thickened and smooth. Add salt, pepper and onion; stir until blended. Set aside to cool. Add zucchini to cooled sauce. Beat egg whites at high speed with cream of tartar until stiff peaks form. Beat yolks until thick and light. Blend in zucchini sauce, then fold mixture into egg whites. Turn into an oiled 1 1/2 quart souffle dish or casserole. Sprinkle with grated cheese. Set in pan containing 1 inch hot water. Bake 1 hour at 350 degrees F. Serve immediately.

Preparation time: 1 hour 40 minutes   Yield: 6 servings

Mary G. Bratt
Waldo, Ohio


## QUICK ZUCCHINI

3 medium zucchini, grated
1/2 c. chopped onion

1 Tbsp. melted butter or margarine
Salt and pepper

Place grated zucchini and onion in skillet with melted butter. Stir and toss over medium high heat for about two minutes. Season to taste with salt and pepper; serve immediately.

Preparation time: 5 minutes          Yield: 4 servings

Mrs. Monroe Dunn
Belzoni, Mississippi


## POTATOES ROMANOFF

6 large potatoes,
   cooked and cubed
2 c. cottage cheese
1 c. sour cream
1-2 cloves garlic, finely diced

1 tsp. salt
2-3 scallions, finely chopped
1 c. grated Cheddar cheese
Paprika

Mix all ingredients except cheese and paprika in casserole. Top with cheese and paprika. Bake at 350 degrees for 30 minutes.

Preparation time: 45 minutes         Yield: 6-8 servings

Claudia Tanner
Eaton Rapids, Michigan

# CHEDDAR SQUASH BAKE

2 lb. summer squash or
   3-4 c. cooked squash
2 slightly beaten eggs
1 c. sour cream (or part yogurt,
   part sour cream, but best
   with all sour cream)

1 small onion, chopped
2 Tbsp. unbleached flour
1 1/2 c. shredded Cheddar (sharp)
   cheese
4 slices bacon, cooked and
   crumbled

    Cook squash; add chopped onion and cook. Add eggs to sour cream plus 2 tablespoons flour. Layer: 1/2 squash, onion, 1/2 sour cream and eggs and 1/2 Cheddar cheese. Repeat layers and garnish with bacon. Bake at 350 degrees for 20-25 minutes.

Preparation time: 35-40 minutes    Yield: 6-8 servings

Diane McLean
Knoxville, Tennessee


# SQUASH DRESSING

2 lb. squash
1/2 c. whole wheat flour
2 tsp. baking powder
1/4 tsp. salt
1/2 c. stone ground corn meal
1 egg
1/2 c. milk

2 Tbsp. oil
2 c. milk
1/2 c. each of chopped celery,
   onion and green pepper
1 can cream of chicken soup
   (check label for ingredients)
1 tsp. sage

    Steam squash, set aside. Make corn bread using flour, baking powder, salt, corn meal, egg, 1/2 cup milk and oil. Bake in greased 8 or 9-inch pan at 425 degrees for 20 minutes. Crumble into 2 cups milk. Mash squash. Add corn bread to squash. Saute vegetables. Add vegetables, soup and sage to squash mixture. Mix well. Bake at 350 degrees for 1 hour or until done. Cheese may be added, if desired. Is easily reheated.

Preparation time: 1 hour 45 minutes   Yield: 6-8 servings

Linda Campbell
Carlton, Texas

## POTATO CASSEROLE WITH SOUR CREAM

6 medium potatoes
  cooked
1 c. grated Gruyere (Swiss)
  or Cheddar cheese
1 Tbsp. butter

2 eggs
1 c. sour cream
1/2 c. milk (or light cream)
1/4 c. chopped fresh parsley
Salt and pepper to taste

Peel cooked potatoes, then slice them. With the butter, grease generously the casserole dish. Put one layer of potatoes, one layer of grated Gruyere. Repeat as needed. Mix the eggs, sour cream, milk, parsley, pepper and salt until smooth. Pour this mixture on top of the potatoes. Cook 1/2 hour at 350 degrees, covered. To brown top, you can take the lid off for the last 10 minutes. You can add or decrease the quantity of milk to suit your taste. Do not forget the parsley, it enhances the flavor.

Preparation time: 1 hour          Yield: 6 servings
    Hint: Potatoes should not be overcooked so they do not fall apart during cooking process.

Lise Stevens
Gainesville, Missouri


## HERBED LENTILS AND RICE

2 2/3 c. broth
3/4 c. lentils
3/4 c. chopped onion
1/2 c. brown rice
1/4 c. dry white wine, optional
1/4 tsp. dry basil

1/4 tsp. salt
1/4 tsp. oregano
1/4 tsp. thyme
1/4 tsp. garlic
1/4 tsp. pepper
4 oz. Swiss cheese

Combine all ingredients except cheese. Shred half of cheese and stir into mixture; turn into ungreased 1 1/2 quart casserole. Bake, covered, in a 350 degree oven for 1 1/2 - 2 hours (stir twice). Slice rest of cheese and top casserole the last few minutes of baking.

Preparation time: 2 - 2 1/2 hours     Yield: 6 servings

Terry L. Praznik
Prairie Village, Kansas

# INDONESIAN RICE

**3-4 c. hot cooked brown rice**
**1/2 c. coarsely chopped salted**
  **peanuts**
**1/4 c. melted butter**

**1/4 c. mild honey**
**1 tsp. cinnamon**
**Minced fresh parsley or green**
  **onions for garnish**

Combine hot rice, peanuts, butter, honey, and cinnamon. Toss gently and quickly and pour into a 2 quart casserole. Cover and keep warm until serving. Just before serving, sprinkle garnish on top.

Preparation time: 5 minutes      Yield: 6-8 servings
Hint: If you start this recipe by cooking the rice, allow 45-50 minutes for the cooking time.

Judy Aversa
Fontana, California

MAIN DISHES

## CHEESE RICE CASSEROLE

1 c. brown rice
3/4 lb. Monterey Jack
  cheese, grated

3/4 c. sharp Cheddar cheese,
  grated
1 (4 oz.) can green chilies, chopped

Cook rice according to package directions. Mix in remaining ingredients, saving a little grated cheese to top the casserole. Bake at 350 degrees for 40 minutes.

Preparation time: 1 hour 45 minutes  Yield: 6 servings
  Hint: To save time, I often plan my menus so that I have rice left over from another meal. That saves cooking time in this recipe.

Judy Beemer
Sharon Springs, Kansas

## CROCK POT BEANS

2 c. dried beans, any kind
1 qt. water

1 Tbsp. honey
1 tsp. salt

The night before serving, place rinsed beans and water in the cold crock pot and cover. In the morning, add honey and salt, cover, and turn on high. (If beans have soaked up all the water, add 1 cup more.) They will be tender and delicious by suppertime.

Preparation time: 5 minutes +
  soaking and cooking time

Yield: 1 quart

Suzanne Ratliff
Russellville, Arkansas

# EGGPLANT LASAGNE

2-3 Tbsp. oil
1 eggplant, sliced and peeled
2 Tbsp. butter
1/2 lb. mushrooms, sliced
1 clove garlic, crushed

1 can spaghetti sauce (read labels)
6 oz. Mozzarella cheese
1/4 c. Parmesan cheese
1 c. cottage cheese (or Ricotta)
2 eggs

Saute sliced eggplant in oil. Saute sliced mushrooms in butter, along with garlic. Add spaghetti sauce to mushrooms and simmer. Beat eggs, add to cottage or Ricotta cheese with 1/4 cup Parmesan cheese. Place small amount of sauce in bottom of 9x13 inch pan. Layer eggplant slices, cottage cheese or Ricotta mixture, sauce mixture, and shredded Mozzarella. Top with more grated Parmesan cheese. Bake 20-30 minutes at 350 degrees.

Preparation time: 45 minutes        Yield: 6-8 servings
    Hint: You may add a touch of red wine to the spaghetti sauce if desired —it is delicious without it.

Carole L. Jasinek
San Diego, California


# VEGETARIAN LASAGNE

10 whole wheat lasagne
   noodles, cooked and drained
2 c. freshly sliced mushrooms
1 c. grated carrots
1/2 c. chopped onion
1 eggplant, sliced and cooked
   or 1 large zucchini, sliced
   and cooked
1 (15 oz.) can tomato sauce
1 (6 oz.) can tomato paste

Oregano, basil and salt to taste
1/2 c. chopped olives
1 large clove garlic, minced
2 c. Ricotta or cottage cheese
2 eggs
16 oz. sliced Monterey Jack
   cheese
1/2 c. Romano or Parmesan
   cheese

Set aside drained pasta. Mix vegetables together in pot. Add tomato paste and sauce. Add a sprinkling of oregano, basil and salt to taste. Add olives and garlic. Simmer 15-20 minutes. Mix together Ricotta and eggs. In a large rectangular dish, place a layer of noodles, then layer 1/2 vegetable mixture and add all cheese mixture. Layer remaining noodles and add remaining vegetable mixture. Top with Monterey Jack cheese. Sprinkle freshly grated Romano or Parmesan cheese on top of this. Bake at 375 degrees for 30 minutes. Let stand before cutting.

Preparation time: 1 hour        Yield: 8-10 servings

Diane McLean
Knoxville, Tennessee

# FLORENTINE CREPE CUPS

**Crepes:**

3 eggs, slightly beaten
2/3 c. unbleached flour

1/2 tsp. salt
1 c. milk

Combine and beat until smooth. Let stand 30 minutes.

**Filling:**

1 1/2 c. shredded sharp
  Cheddar cheese
3 Tbsp. unbleached flour
3 eggs, slightly beaten
2/3 c. homemade mayonnaise
10 oz. pkg. frozen chopped
  spinach, thawed and drained

4 oz. can mushrooms,
  drained
6 pieces cooked, crumbled
  bacon
1/2 tsp. salt
Dash of black pepper

Toss cheese with flour. Add other ingredients; mix well.

Pour 2 tablespoons crepe batter into hot, lightly greased (non-stick) skillet. Cook on one side only until lightly browned. Fit crepes (browned side down) into greased muffin pan. Fill with cheese mixture. Bake at 350 degrees for 40 minutes or until set. Garnish with bacon bits if desired.

Preparation time: 1 hour 15 minutes   Yield: 12 crepe cups

Hint: Use soy-bacon bits, or watch for fresh frozen bacon, free of sugar or nitrates.

Karen Reynolds
Siloam Springs, Arkansas


# BAKED OMELET

4 eggs
1 c. milk
1 Tbsp. unbleached flour

Pinch salt
1 c. chopped ham or crumbled
  bacon

Beat eggs; add milk, flour and salt. Add meat. Put in buttered 8-inch square pan or quart casserole. Bake 30 minutes at 350 degrees.

Preparation time: 40 minutes       Yield: 3-4 servings

Mrs. George Dixon
Milford, Illinois

## QUICK MICROWAVE CASSEROLE

1-2 Tbsp. butter or margarine
1/4 c. chopped onion (more if
  desired)
5-6 fresh mushrooms, sliced

1/2 c. cooked brown rice
1/2 c. grated Cheddar cheese
1 Tbsp. unhulled sesame seeds
1 Tbsp. walnuts, coarsely broken

Saute onion in butter; add mushrooms. Remove from heat. Reserving small amount of cheese, mix all ingredients. Place in individual casserole. Top with remaining cheese. Microwave 2 minutes on slow-cook setting.

Preparation time: 10 minutes       Yield: 1 serving
  Hint: To cook conventionally, place in 350 degree oven for 15-20 minutes.

Janet Redding
Pasadena, California

## WHOLE WHEAT VEGETARIAN PIE

1 c. whole wheat flour
1 c. unbleached flour
1 tsp. salt
2/3 c. butter or margarine
5-7 Tbsp. cold water
1 c. chopped zucchini
1 c. chopped celery
1/2 c. shredded carrots
1/2 c. sliced mushrooms
1/2 c. chopped green pepper
1 clove garlic, minced
2 Tbsp. oil

2 c. pureed tomatoes
1/2 c. cooked cut green beans
1/2 c. cooked whole kernel corn
1 tsp. dried oregano
1 tsp. chili powder
1/2 tsp. salt
1/2 tsp. dried basil
1/4 tsp. pepper
1/4 tsp. ground allspice
1 c. shredded Cheddar cheese
1 beaten egg

Stir together flours and 1 teaspoon salt. Cut in butter until pieces are pea-sized. Sprinkle water, 1 tablespoon at a time, tossing mixture after each addition. Form into 2 balls. Roll one ball to 1/8 inch thickness; fit into 9-inch pie plate, trim.

In a skillet, saute zucchini, celery, carrots, mushrooms, green pepper and garlic in the hot oil until tender. Add tomato puree, beans, corn and seasonings. Simmer, uncovered, 5 minutes. Spoon into shell. Sprinkle with cheese. Roll out remaining pastry for top crust, seal edge and crimp; cut vents in top. Beat egg and 1 tablespoon water together; brush over crust. Cover edges with foil. Bake at 350 degrees for 20 minutes. Remove foil. Bake another 20-25 minutes; let stand 10-15 minutes before serving.

Preparation time: 1 1/2 hours       Yield: 6 generous servings

Terry L. Praznik
Prairie Village, Kansas

# UNUSUAL YUMMY SOUP

1/3 c. butter or margarine
2 onions, sliced in rings
3/4 tsp. salt
1/2 tsp. pepper

1 Tbsp. flour
1 (13 oz.) can evaporated milk
2/3 c. alfalfa sprouts

Melt butter or margarine in saucepan and saute onions until tender. Add flour, salt and pepper. Cook, stirring constantly, for 1 minute. Add milk and stir until slightly thickened, then add sprouts and stir constantly for one more minute or until thoroughly heated through. Serve immediately.

Preparation time: 10 minutes     Yield: 4 servings

Lou Sutton
Harrison, Arkansas

# CREAM OF PUMPKIN (OR SQUASH) SOUP

4 Tbsp. butter
4 Tbsp. dry minced onion
2 Tbsp. whole wheat flour
2 c. chicken or vegetable broth
2 c. mashed pumpkin or
   butternut squash (blend in blender)

2 c. milk
2 c. light cream
1/2 tsp. marjoram
1 tsp. salt
1/2 tsp. pepper

Saute onion in butter. Add flour and slowly stir in the broth. Heat and stir until slightly thickened. Add pumpkin, milk, cream, and seasonings. Simmer 15 minutes.

Preparation time: 45 minutes     Yield: 8 servings

Mrs. James Anderson
Rock Falls, Illinois

# BROCCOLI SOUP

1 bunch broccoli, washed
   trimmed and chopped
1 stalk celery, chopped
1 small onion, finely minced

3 c. chicken stock (can use
   canned Swanson)
1/8 tsp. dry mustard
1/8 tsp. salt
1 c. light cream

Bring all ingredients to a boil and simmer 15 minutes. Pour soup in blender, add dry mustard and salt. Blend with one cup light cream. Warm slightly and serve with croutons.

Preparation time: 15 minutes     Yield: 1 1/2 quarts

Margriet Olson
Marcus, Iowa

## POTATO DUMPLING SOUP

1 1/2 c. chopped celery
1 1/2 c. chopped carrots
1 c. chopped onion
1/4 c. chopped parsley
2 Tbsp. salt
4 qt. hot water
1/2 c. melted butter or margarine

1/2 c. unbleached flour
1 1/2 tsp. paprika
1/2 tsp. onion salt
1 can chicken broth
1 (6 oz.) can tomato juice
4 c. diced peeled potatoes

Combine first six ingredients in an 8-quart kettle. Make a paste of butter, flour, paprika, and onion salt. Add to kettle mixture and bring to a boil. Add chicken broth and tomato juice; cook and simmer 1 hour. Add 4 cups potatoes and simmer for 2 more hours. Assemble ingredients and make dumplings as directed below.

**Dumplings:**

2 eggs
1/2 tsp. salt

3/4 tsp. baking powder
1 c. unbleached flour
Milk

Mix ingredients with enough milk to make dumplings. Drop from teaspoon into bubbling soup and cook, covered, 15 minutes; uncover and cook an additional 15 minutes.

Preparation time: 4 hours          Yield: 12-14 servings

Mrs. William Umbel
Boardman, Ohio

## POTATO CHOWDER

5 large potatoes
4 oz. cooked ham, shredded
1 medium onion, chopped
1 Tbsp. fresh parsley, minced

1 pt. whole milk
Salt and pepper
2 Tbsp. butter
2 Tbsp. wholegrain flour

Peel and dice potatoes; cover with cold water. Brown ham and onion together. Drain excess water from diced potatoes and layer in a stewing kettle: potatoes, ham, onion, and parsley, repeating until all is used. Cover with cold water and bring to a slow boil, cooking until potatoes are just tender. Add the milk and heat to boiling over low heat. Season to taste with salt and pepper. Make a paste of the butter and flour; stir into the chowder and continue cooking gently until it bubbles and thickens.

Preparation time: 30 minutes          Yield: 6 servings

Blonde Mynatt
Luttrell, Tennessee

## BEEF BARLEY SOUP
### "Delicious and Nutritious - a thicker soup"

14 c. hot water
6 short ribs of beef
1 c. corn
1 c. chopped celery
1/2 c. chopped onion
1/3 c. barley
3 large diced carrots

3 large diced and peeled
  tomatoes
1/4 c. dried split peas
1/4 c. dried lima beans
1/4 c. dried Northern beans
2 Tbsp. chopped parsley
1 Tbsp. salt

Bring water and ribs to a boil in an 8-quart kettle. Remove foam with a strainer until broth is clear. Add remaining ingredients and lower the heat. Simmer 3 1/2 - 4 hours with lid tipped. Remove meat from bones, shred and return to soup. May season with additional salt and pepper if desired.

Preparation time: 4 1/2 hours          Yield: 4 quarts

Mr. and Mrs. William Umbel
Boardman, Ohio


## HEARTY VEGETABLE SOUP

2 c. dried beans
6 c. water
1 chopped onion
1 c. chopped celery
3 Tbsp. soy sauce (Tamari™)
3 Tbsp. vinegar

1/2 c. sliced carrots
1 c. chopped cabbage
2 cloves garlic, minced
1/4 c. uncooked rice or barley
1/2 lb. ground beef, browned
2 Tbsp. cornstarch

Soak beans overnight in water to cover. Pour off water. Add 6 cups water and remaining ingredients except cornstarch. Thicken with cornstarch when all vegetables are tender. Add salt if needed.

Preparation time: overnight +          Yield: 8 generous servings
                3 hours
Hint: Can substitute 3 bouillon cubes for the ground beef or use leftover chicken or beef.

Mrs. Charles F. Morgan
Knoxville, Tennessee

## LENTIL & BEEF SOUP

1 lb. lean beef for stew
3 Tbsp. unbleached flour
2 tsp. salt
1/4 tsp. pepper
3 Tbsp. oil
5 c. water
2 c. sliced celery

5 medium carrots, thinly sliced
2 large onions, chopped
1 c. lentils
1 Tbsp. lemon juice
1 1/2 tsp. salt
1 tsp. thyme

Cut beef into 1/2 inch pieces. Combine flour, 2 teaspoons salt and pepper; dredge meat. Brown beef in oil in Dutch oven. Add water, cover and simmer for 45 minutes. Stir in celery, carrots, onions, lentils, lemon juice, salt and thyme. Simmer, covered, 1 hour; stir occasionally.

Preparation time: 2 hours 20 minutes Yield: 8 servings

Gloria Dooley
Wynne, Arkansas

## CHICKEN GUMBO

3 chicken breasts
1 c. uncooked brown rice
4 c. broth, from cooked
    chicken
1 c. chopped onion
1 Tbsp. unbleached flour

1 Tbsp. oil
1 Tbsp. file' powder
2 qt. canned tomatoes
1/2 c. okra, sliced thin
1 can cream of chicken soup
    (optional)

Simmer chicken until done in 6-8 cups water; bone and shred. Cook rice in 3 cups water until done. Combine in a large pot: chicken with 4 cups broth, onion, flour, (blend in), oil, file' powder, tomatoes and okra. Simmer for 45 minutes, stirring often. The last ten minutes, add the cooked rice and cream of chicken soup; stir to blend and add salt to taste.

Preparation time: 2 hours          Yield: 4 quarts
    Hint: This freezes well — is even better the day after cooking.

Carol Ashberry
Cabot, Arkansas

## BLISS' OYSTER ARTICHOKE SOUP

1 bunch green onions, chopped
Thyme, cayenne, salt to taste
3 bay leaves
2/3 stick butter
2 Tbsp. whole grain flour
1 can chicken broth

2 c. oyster water
2 c. oysters, cut up
1 can artichoke hearts, chopped
3 sprigs parsley
1/2 c. whipping cream

Saute green onions, thyme, cayenne, salt and bay leaves in butter. Add flour; whisk well. Add broth and oyster water. Simmer 15 minutes. Add oysters, artichokes, and parsley. Simmer 10 minutes; add cream. Serve.

Preparation time: 1 hour          Yield: 4 to 6 servings

Betsy Branstetter
Kansas City, Missouri


## SWEET AND SOUR SHRIMP

1 box long grain and wild rice
3 c. shrimp, cooked
4 Tbsp. butter or margarine
1 green pepper, cut in strips
1 small jar pimentoes
1 can water chestnuts, sliced
2 1/2 c. unsweetened pineapple
   chunks

1/2 c. vinegar
1/2 c. honey
1 Tbsp. soy sauce
1/4 c. unbleached flour
2 tsp. ginger
1/4 tsp. salt

Cook rice according to directions on box. Meanwhile, saute the shrimp in butter about 3 minutes, stirring occasionally. Drain pineapple into a pint measuring cup. To the pineapple juice, add honey, vinegar and soy sauce. Remove shrimp and use the remaining butter with the flour to make a paste, cooking until blended; add the liquid mixture and cook until clear and thickened. Add ginger and salt. Add shrimp, green pepper, pimentoes, water chestnuts and pineapple chunks and heat thoroughly yet leaving the green pepper slightly crisp....about 2 minutes. Serve shrimp mixture with rice.

Preparation time: 30-35 minutes          Yield: 6 servings

Mrs. Carl F. Maples, Sr.
Knoxville, Tennessee

**Ed. Note:** Try this one for sure....my mom sent it in....mmmm.

# BAKED FISH

| | |
|---|---|
| 2 lb. fresh or partially thawed fish fillets | 3 oz. cream cheese |
| | 1/2 c. sour cream |
| 1/4 c. homemade mayonnaise | 1 tsp. dried dill weed (optional) |

Cut fish into serving size pieces and place in a buttered baking dish. Mix the remaining ingredients until smooth and cover fish. Bake, uncovered, at 350 degrees for about 45 minutes.

Preparation time: 50 minutes    Yield: 4 servings

Linda Olson
Big Rock, Illinois

# TUNA-CHEESE QUICHE

**Pastry for 9-inch pie:**

| | |
|---|---|
| 1 1/3 c. unbleached or whole wheat flour | 3 Tbsp. butter or margarine |
| | 3 Tbsp. oil |
| Pinch salt | 2-5 Tbsp. cold milk |

Cut butter, oil and salt into flour until mealy. Add milk, a tablespoon at a time, until dough gathers in a ball. Roll between 2 sheets of waxed paper. Line pan and prick sides with fork.

**Custard:**

| | |
|---|---|
| 1 1/4 c. milk, half and half, or cream | 2 egg yolks |
| 1 whole egg | Pinch each of salt, cayenne, nutmeg |

Whip together.

**Filling:**

| | |
|---|---|
| 1 (7 oz.) can tuna, water pack, drained | 1/2 c. cubed cheese, (Colby, Cheddar, Mozzarella or whatever) |

Break up tuna and spread on bottom of prepared pie shell. Scatter cheese over tuna. Pour custard over tuna and cheese. Bake in preheated oven at 375 degrees for 35-45 minutes or until custard is puffed up and slightly browned. Let rest for 5 minutes before cutting.

Preparation time: 1 hour    Yield: One 9-inch pie

Kathi McCallum
Franktown, Colorado

# TUNA BURGERS

1 (6 1/2 oz.) can tuna, drained
1 egg, slightly beaten
1/2 c. wholegrain bread crumbs
1 Tbsp. wheat germ
1 Tbsp. homemade mayonnaise
1 tsp. dill or honey sweetened
  relish

1/4 tsp. onion salt
1 tsp. lemon juice
Dash of Worcestershire sauce
  (optional)
Dash of pepper
2 Tbsp. butter or margarine

Mix ingredients except butter, in a bowl. Toss lightly with a fork and shape into patties. Coat patties in additional bread crumbs if desired. Cover and refrigerate until ready to cook, or cook immediately; as desired. Melt butter in a skillet, brown on each side.

Preparation time: 15 minutes        Yield: 3 burgers
    Hint: Melt a little cheese on top for an extra special treat.

Mrs. William Umbel
Boardman, Ohio


# TUNA-NOODLE CASSEROLE

6 oz. (3 c.) whole wheat
  noodles
6 1/2 - 7 oz. can tuna, drained
1/2 c. homemade mayonnaise
1 c. chopped celery
1/3 c. chopped onion
1/4 c. chopped green pepper

1/4 c. chopped pimento
1/2 tsp. salt
1/2 c. peas (optional)
1 (10 oz.) can mushroom soup
1/2 c. milk
4 oz. sharp cheese, shredded
Slivered almonds or whole
  wheat Chinese noodles

Cook whole wheat noodles; drain. Combine noodles, tuna, mayonnaise, celery, onion, green pepper, pimento, and salt. Add peas, if desired. Blend cream of mushroom soup and milk; heat through. Add sharp cheese; heat and stir until cheese melts. Add all to noodle mixture; turn into 2-quart casserole. Top with slivered almonds or whole wheat Chinese noodles if desired. Bake, uncovered, at 425 degrees for 20 minutes.

Preparation time: 45 minutes        Yield: 6 servings

Kathy Ortmann
Marcus, Iowa

# QUICHE

1 whole wheat pie crust
6 beaten eggs
1 c. half & half

1 c. Jack, Swiss or Cheddar cheese
1 c. onion, vegetable, meat, fish,
    chicken, or any combination of
    these

Brush pie crust with beaten egg and bake at 450 degrees for 10 minutes. Beat eggs, half & half, salt and pepper to taste. Mix cheese and meat mixture and put into pie shell. Pour eggs over meat mixture. Bake at 350 degrees about 45 minutes or until toothpick comes out clean in center. Cool 10 minutes and serve.

Preparation time: 1 1/2 hours        Yield: 4-6 servings

Christine Kenshalo
Kenai, Alaska

# SALMON QUICHE

1 c. whole wheat flour
2/3 c. grated Cheddar cheese
1/4 c. chopped almonds
1/2 tsp. salt
1/4 tsp. paprika
6 Tbsp. oil
3 eggs, beaten
1 c. sour cream

1/4 c. mayonnaise
1/2 c. grated Cheddar cheese
1 Tbsp. grated onion
1/4 tsp. dill weed
3 drops hot sauce
1 (15 oz.) can salmon, drained,
    boned, and flaked (save juice)

Combine first 5 ingredients in a bowl; add oil and toss; press firmly in a 9-inch pie plate, reserving 1/2 cup for topping. Bake 10 minutes at 400 degrees. Combine eggs, sour cream and mayonnaise; mix until smooth. Add remaining ingredients except salmon to the egg mixture; add salmon juice and water to make 1/2 cup liquid. Stir in salmon, pour into crust, and top with reserved crumbs. Bake 45-55 minutes at 325 degrees or until filling is solid.

Preparation time: 1 hour 15 minutes   Yield: 4-6 servings

Linda Olson
Big Rock, Illinois

# CHICKEN QUICHE

1 (9-inch) unbaked pie crust
  (made with unbleached flour)
1 c. finely cubed cooked
  chicken
3 oz. grated Edam cheese
3 eggs
1 Tbsp. flour

1 1/2 c. milk
Dash nutmeg
1/2 tsp. salt
1/8 tsp. pepper
1 Tbsp. onion flakes
1 Tbsp. chopped Bell pepper
1 Tbsp. melted butter or margarine

Sprinkle chicken, then cheese into pastry shell. Beat eggs slightly; stir in flour, milk, seasonings, and butter or margarine. Pour over chicken and cheese. Bake in 425 degree oven for 15 minutes; then reduce oven temperature to 375 degrees for 20 minutes. Cool for 5 minutes before cutting.

Preparation time: 1 hour        Yield: 6 servings

Judy Harned
Coyle, Oklahoma


# CHICKEN AND PEPPER SKILLET

2 whole large chicken breasts
3 Tbsp. soy sauce
2 tsp. cornstarch
1/8 tsp. garlic powder
1/8 tsp. fructose
5 Tbsp. oil

2 medium green or red peppers
1/2 c. chopped celery
1/2 c. onion strips
1/2 c. bean sprouts
1/2 c. water

Cut chicken breasts in halves, remove skin and bones. Slice across width of each half into 1/8 inch thick slices. Mix chicken, soy sauce, cornstarch, garlic powder and fructose. Set aside. Cut green peppers into 1/4 inch wide strips. In 12-inch skillet over medium high heat in 2 tablespoons hot salad oil, stir fry peppers, celery, onions and bean sprouts, stirring quickly and frequently, until crisp-tender....about 2 minutes. With slotted spoon remove vegetables to bowl. In same skillet over high heat, in 3 more tablespoons hot oil, cook chicken mixture, stirring quickly and frequently, until chicken is tender, about 5 minutes. Return vegetables to skillet. Add water; heat to boiling, stirring to loosen brown bits from bottom of skillet. Serve over rice.

Preparation time: 20 minutes     Yield: 4 servings
   Hint: This recipe works nicely in a Wok.

Mary Lu Wheeler
Willard, Missouri

## CHEESY CHICKEN CASSEROLE

1 (4 lb.) chicken or 3 breasts
2 (10 oz) pkg. frozen broccoli
2 c. milk
2 (8 oz.) pkg. cream cheese

1 tsp. salt
3/4 - 1 tsp. garlic salt
1 1/2 c. Parmesan cheese, shredded

Simmer chicken in seasoned water until tender. Let cool, remove skin and slice thinly. Refrigerate. About 1 hour before serving, cook broccoli as directed on package. Cut in bite-size pieces and place in buttered 2-quart oblong baking dish.

Blend milk, cream cheese, salt and garlic salt, stirring constantly over heat until smooth. Stir in 3/4 cup Parmesan cheese and heat until smooth and creamy. Pour 1 cup of sauce over broccoli, then top with all the chicken in one layer. Cover chicken with rest of sauce. Sprinkle 1/4 cup Parmesan cheese over top. Bake at 350 degrees for 30 minutes. Serve with rest of shredded cheese.

Preparation time:
      Chicken - 2 1/2 hours
      Casserole - 1 hour

Yield: 8 servings

Beth Miller
Emporia, Kansas


## CHICKEN ALMOND BAKE

2 c. cubed cooked chicken
2 c. sliced celery
1/4 c. chopped onion
3/4 c. homemade mayonnaise
1/3 c. slivered almonds

3 Tbsp. lemon juice
1/2 tsp. salt
1/4 c. sunflower seeds
1/4 c. alfalfa sprouts
3/4 c. shredded cheese
1 c. crushed potato chips

Combine all the above ingredients except shredded cheese and potato chips and pile lightly in 9-inch square casserole dish. Sprinkle with shredded cheese and top with 1 cup crushed potato chips. Cover and bake at 425 degrees for 20 minutes or microwave on high for 5 minutes.

Preparation time: Mixing 10
            minutes

Yield: 6 servings

Lou Sutton
Harrison, Arkansas

# HONEYED CHICKEN

1 broiler chicken, cut up
  for frying
4 Tbsp. unbleached flour
2 tsp. salt

2 tsp. paprika
1/4 tsp. pepper
1/2 c. butter

**Honey Butter Coating:**

1/4 c. lemon juice
1/4 c. honey

1/4 c. melted butter or margarine

Mix well.

Dip chicken pieces in mixture of flour, salt, paprika and pepper. Coat with butter and bake in shallow baking pan in oven at 400 degrees for 30 minutes. Turn chicken and then pour Honey-Butter Sauce over chicken. Bake another 30 minutes or until tender. Baste from time to time and watch carefully as honey tends to burn. May have to turn oven down to 300 degrees and bake a little longer.

Preparation time: 1 1/2 hours          Yield: 6-8 servings

Shirley Nickels
Vancouver, Washington


# CHICKEN CHILI

1 (3 lb.) chicken
2 cans cream of chicken soup
1 soup can milk
2 medium onions, chopped

2 cans green chilies, chopped
1 lb. grated Cheddar cheese
12 corn tortillas

Boil chicken until tender; bone and cut into pieces. In a large bowl mix boned chicken, soup, milk, onions and chilies. In a 9x13-inch pan, layer 6 tortillas, half the chicken mixture, half the cheese; repeat. Bake at 350 degrees 40-45 minutes or until bubbly and done.

Preparation time: 3 1/2 - 4 hours          Yield: 12-14 servings
    (1 hour if starting with boned
    chicken)
    Hint: You may want to reduce the amount of chilies.

Mrs. Norman E. Lemay
North Glenn, Colorado

# RUTH'S CHICKEN

6 chicken breasts
6 Tbsp. butter or margarine
Salt, pepper and paprika
  to taste
1 can artichoke hearts
2 Tbsp. wholegrain flour

1 large can mushrooms
1/2 c. chopped green onions
2/3 c. chicken broth
1/4 c. cooking sherry
1/2 tsp. rosemary

Melt butter in a heavy skillet; add chicken, seasoned with salt, pepper, and paprika. Place in a casserole and arrange artichoke hearts around chicken. Add wholegrain flour to the butter in the skillet, cook and stir to make a roux. Add mushrooms and onions and saute; then stir in broth, cooking sherry and rosemary. Cook 5 minutes over low heat to blend and thicken, then pour sauce over chicken. Bake, uncovered, for 1 hour at 375 degrees.

Preparation time: 1 hour 30 minutes   Yield: 6 servings

Betsy Branstetter
Kansas City, Missouri


# CHICKEN CHOW MEIN

2 Tbsp. fat (from boiled chicken)
3 c. diced boiled chicken
4 c. shredded cabbage
1 stalk celery, diced
1 carrot, thinly sliced

1 can water chestnuts, sliced
1 1/2 c. chicken broth (excess
  fat skimmed off)
3 Tbsp. cornstarch
3 Tbsp. water
3 Tbsp. soy sauce

Place first seven ingredients in a frypan and cook 10 minutes with a cover. Then make a well in the center of this and add: cornstarch, water, and soy sauce.
Let this begin to thicken, then serve over crisp noodles or brown rice.

Preparation time: 20 minutes        Yield: 6-8 servings

Marcella Brown
Marcus, Iowa

## ESCALLOPED CHICKEN

| | |
|---|---|
| 1 cut-up frying chicken | 2 c. corn bread crumbs |
| 1 stick butter, melted | 1/2 c. celery |
| 1/2 c. unbleached flour | 1/4 c. onions |
| 2 c. chicken broth | 1/4 tsp. sage |
| 1 c. milk | 1/4 c. melted butter |
| Salt and pepper to taste | Paprika |

Boil chicken in salt water until done. Remove bone. Blend butter, flour, broth and milk in saucepan and cook 2-3 minutes until thick. Season with salt and pepper. Combine corn bread, celery, onions, sage and butter; mix well. Arrange dressing in baking dish, place chicken pieces on top and cover with sauce. Sprinkle with paprika. Bake at 350 degrees for one hour.

Preparation time: 1 1/2 - 2 hours     Yield: 4-6 servings

Kathy Horton
Ocean Springs, Mississippi

## CHICKEN ENCHILADA CASSEROLE

| | |
|---|---|
| 6 Tbsp. butter or margarine | 1/2 c. chopped onion |
| 6 Tbsp. whole wheat flour | Tortillas |
| 3 c. chicken broth | 2 c. cooked diced chicken |
| 2-3 tsp. chili powder | 2 c. shredded Cheddar cheese |
| 1 can green chilies, seeded | 1 c. sour cream |
| and diced | |

Make a white sauce by melting butter in a skillet over medium heat, then stirring in flour quickly, heating and stirring until it is bubbly. Add chicken broth, a cup at a time, stirring with a wire whisk to blend. Cook and stir until thickened, then add chili powder, chilies and onions to the sauce. Layer tortillas, sauce, chicken and cheese, ending with cheese on final layer. Top with sour cream, cover, and bake for 30 minutes at 350 degrees.

Preparation time: 45 minutes     Yield: 8 servings

Amy Parry
Ft. Collins, Colorado

## HONEY BARBECUED CHICKEN

1/4 c. butter or margarine
1/2 c. orange juice
1/2 c. honey
2 Tbsp. lemon juice

2 Tbsp. chopped parsley
2 Tbsp. Worcestershire sauce
   (optional)
1 Tbsp. mustard
2 broiler-fryers, split in halves

Melt butter in a small saucepan. Blend in the remaining ingredients and simmer 2-3 minutes. Cool. Put the chicken halves, cavity side down, on grill. Cook slowly 40-45 minutes, basting frequently with sauce. Turn and cook for an additional 10 minutes.

Preparation time: 1 hour          Yield: 6-8 servings

Mrs. Kathy Horton
Ocean Springs, Mississippi


## CHICKEN HAWAIIAN

1 c. whole wheat flour
Salt and pepper
1 egg, beaten lightly
2 whole chicken breasts,
   split, boned and skinned

Oil
1 c. uncooked brown rice
1 fresh pineapple, cubed
1/4 c. honey, warmed

Mix flour, salt, and pepper. Dip chicken into egg and then dredge in flour. Fry in 1/4 inch oil. Turn once.
While chicken is frying, cook rice by bringing water to boil and then adding rice slowly. When rice has finished cooking, drain and add salt to taste, then pineapple. Stir. Simmer 5-10 minutes.
Place rice/pineapple on platter. Cut chicken into bite-size pieces and lay on top of rice. Pour hot honey over chicken and rice.
For a pretty table, cut pineapple in half lengthwise. Scoop out pineapple for rice. Fill cavities of pineapple with rice/pineapple and chicken.

Preparation time: 1 hour 15 minutes   Yield: 4-6 servings

Sue Marie Brown
Nashville, Tennessee

## CHEDDAR CHICKEN OR TURKEY CASSEROLE

1 c. brown rice, uncooked
2 Tbsp. minced onion
1 c. green peas, cooked
  and drained
2 c. cooked chicken or
  turkey

2 c. white sauce (made with whole
  wheat flour)
1/2 c. Cheddar cheese, grated
1 c. finely crumbled natural
  style cheese crackers
3 tsp. melted butter

Cook rice, adding onion to boiling water. Spread rice in oiled baking dish. Sprinkle on peas; cover with chicken or turkey. Melt cheese in white sauce. Pour over chicken or turkey. Combine cracker crumbs and melted butter. Sprinkle on top. Bake 30-35 minutes at 350 degrees.

Preparation time: 1 1/2 hours       Yield: 6-8 servings
    Hint: To make white sauce, melt 2 tablespoons butter in skillet, blend in 2 tablespoons whole wheat flour and cook for one minute; stirring constantly. Add 2 cups milk, stirring as you add with wire whisk. Continue cooking until bubbly and thickened.

Kathleen Hackman
London, Arkansas


## BISCUIT TOPPED TURKEY CASSEROLE

6 medium potatoes, peeled
  and quartered
6 medium carrots, peeled
  and quartered
1/4 c. chopped onion

1/4 c. chopped green pepper
2 Tbsp. butter
1 can cream of mushroom soup
3 c. chopped cooked turkey or
  chicken

Steam potatoes and carrots in a large pan, covered, until tender. Save 1 cup of the liquid from steaming. Saute onions and peppers in butter until softened; stir in the soup and reserved liquid. Spoon vegetables into a 2-quart casserole, gently fold in chopped turkey, and cover with sauce. Bake in a 425 degree oven while you prepare biscuit topping.

**Biscuit Topping:**

3/4 c. whole wheat flour
3/4 c. unbleached flour
2 tsp. baking powder

1/2 tsp. salt
1/4 c. soft butter
1/2 c. milk

Combine dry ingredients, cut in butter until well distributed throughout. Add milk, stir, and knead lightly. Pat or roll out and cut in 1/2-inch rounds. Top casserole with biscuits; bake 15 minutes at 425 degrees.

Preparation time: 1 hour       Yield: 8-10 servings

Janet Campbell
Corvallis, Oregon

# PITA WITH MEAT FILLING

**Pita:**

**1 Tbsp. yeast**                                    **3-4 c. whole wheat flour**
**1 1/4 c. tepid water**

Dissolve the yeast in the tepid water. Stir in 2 cups flour, beat 50 strokes to work up the gluten and add air. Add the rest of the flour a half cup at a time until the dough comes away from the sides of the bowl. Knead the dough in the bowl or on a floured board for 10 minutes. Add flour if needed until dough is elastic and smooth and no longer sticks to your fingers. Shape dough into 10 balls about 2 inches in diameter. Roll out into a round 5 inches across and 1/4 inch thick. Let rise 15 minutes or until slightly risen. Turn rounds upside down on an unoiled baking sheet. Place in a 500 degree oven on the bottom rack. Bake 5 minutes until they are well puffed. They are hard but will soften as they cool.

Preparation time: 1 hour                    Yield: 10 pitas

**Meat Filling:**

**1 1/2 lb. raw turkey or rabbit**                **2 c. cooked pinto beans**
  **(grind in meat grinder)**                        **1 1/2 c. cheese**
**1 Tbsp. oil**
**1 1/2 - 2 Tbsp. chili powder**

Saute ground turkey or rabbit in oil in skillet; stir until pinkness disappears. Stir in chili powder and pinto beans. Cook 3 minutes until hot. Blend cheese into mixture, stir until melted. Slice pitas halfway through and the bread forms a pocket. Stuff with the filling.

Preparation time: 30 minutes              Yield: Stuffing for 10 pitas

Linda Campbell
Carlton, Texas

# LENTIL STEW

| | |
|---|---|
| 1 c. lentils | 1 medium onion, chopped |
| 2 1/2 c. water | 1 clove garlic, minced |
| 2 beef bouillon cubes | 3/4 c. tomato paste |
| 1 bay leaf | 2 stalks celery, chopped |
| 1 tsp. salt | 5 c. water |
| 1/2 lb. ground beef | 1/4 tsp. oregano |
| | 1 tsp. salt |

Bring to a boil: lentils, water, bouillon cubes, bay leaf and salt; reduce heat and simmer, covered, 20 minutes. Meanwhile, brown ground beef with onion and garlic. Add to lentils along with remaining ingredients. Bring to a boil, reduce heat and simmer, covered, for 30 minutes. Serve plain or over rice.

Preparation time: 1 hour          Yield: 6 servings
    Hint: You may want to use 2 1/2 cups canned or homemade beef broth to avoid the small amount of sugar in the cubes.

Mrs. James Anderson
Rock Falls, Illinois

# BEEF VEGETABLE (YORKSHIRE) PUDDING

| | |
|---|---|
| 1 Tbsp. oil | Pinch pepper |
| 1 small onion, sliced thinly | 2 Tbsp. unbleached flour |
| 1 - 1 1/2 lb. lean ground chuck | 3-5 Tbsp. water |
| 3/4 c. cooked mixed | 2 Tbsp. oil |
|   vegetables (leftovers) | 1 c. unbleached flour |
| Sliced mushrooms (optional) | 1/2 tsp. salt |
| 1 (14 oz.) can tomatoes | 2 eggs |
| 1/2 tsp. salt | 1 c. milk |

Preheat oven to 425 degrees. Saute onion in oil in a large skillet. Break up meat and brown with onion. Drain excess oil. Add vegetables, tomatoes and seasonings. Mix well. Bring to a boil. Make a paste of 2 tablespoons flour and water and stir briskly into boiling meat mixture to thicken. Put 2 tablespoons of oil in a 10-inch quiche dish or pie plate—at least 2 1/2 - 3 inches deep or deeper. Put into hot oven to heat. While heating, blend remaining flour, eggs, milk and salt to make batter. Beat until smooth. (A wire wisk is great for this type of mixing). Pour batter into heated dish. Spoon meat mixture over batter evenly to within 1 inch of edge. Bake at 400 degrees for 30 minutes or until pudding is brown and puffy. Yorkshire pudding will puff all around edge forming delicious bottom crust.

Preparation time: 1 hour          Yield: 1 quiche or 10-inch pie
    Hint: Great one dish meal when served with cheese and cole slaw or tossed salad.

Marsha Hills
Peace River, Alberta, Canada

# MICROWAVED PIZZA WITH WHOLE WHEAT CRUST

**Crust:**

1 c. whole wheat flour
1 c. unbleached flour
2 tsp. baking powder

2/3 c. milk
6 Tbsp. oil

**Sauce:**

8 oz. can tomato sauce
1/4 c. homemade catsup
1/4 c. chopped onion

1 1/2 tsp. oregano leaves
1/2 tsp. leaf basil
1/4 tsp. garlic powder

**Topping:**

1/2 c. Parmesan cheese
2 c. drained sauerkraut

2 c. cooked hamburger meat (1/2
   lb. drained, seasoned to taste)
3 c. shredded Mozzarella cheese

Combine flours and baking powder in mixing bowl. Stir in milk and oil until dough leaves sides of bowl and forms a ball. Knead 4 or 5 times; shape into a ball (two balls preferred). Place ball of dough between squares of waxed paper. Roll to an 11-inch circle. Peel off top sheet of waxed paper. Place dough (still on waxed paper) on oven rack or inserted microwave roasting rack. Microwave on high for 4 minutes, uncovered. Invert dough then carefully peel off waxed paper. Microwave on high for 1/2 - 2 minutes or until dough is no longer doughy. Remove crust from oven, leaving it on the rack. Combine ingredients for sauce; spoon onto crust, spreading to edges. Sprinkle evenly with the cheese, sauerkraut and meat; place in microwave. Microwave on high for 5 1/2 - 6 minutes, until cheese is melted, rotating pizza once.

Preparation time: 30 minutes          Yield: 8 servings
    Hint: To cook conventionally, bake crust for 10 minutes at 425 degrees; bake assembled pizzas about 10 minutes at 425 degrees or just until cheese is bubbly.

Diane Ruden
Marcus, Iowa

# PIZZA

**Dough:**

1 c. whole wheat flour
1/2 c. wheat germ
3 - 3 1/2 c. unbleached flour
1 pkg. yeast

1 c. buttermilk, heated
  (or 1 c. hot water)
1 Tbsp. butter or margarine

In bowl, stir together whole wheat flour, wheat germ, 1/2 cup unbleached flour and yeast. Meanwhile, heat buttermilk and butter or margarine (it need not melt); add to flour mixture. Beat with mixer until smooth. Add enough unbleached flour to make a stiff dough. Turn out on floured surface and knead. Put in greased bowl and let rise about an hour. (Rising time is not absolutely necessary but the dough is easier to spread on pizza pans if it is allowed to rise for a time.) Grease pizza pans and spread dough (3 pans for thin crust; 2 for thick crust). Add sauce and toppings.

**Italian Sauce (Makes 3 Pizzas):**

1/2 lb. ground pork (or beef)
1 (8 oz.) can tomato sauce

1 Tbsp. Italian seasonings
Dash of garlic powder
3/4 - 1 lb. shredded Mozzarella or
  Muenster cheese

Brown meat and pour off fat. Add tomato sauce, Italian seasonings, and garlic powder and cook slowly until dough is ready.

Pour in thin layer over dough spread on pizza pans. Add 3/4 - 1 pound shredded Mozzarella or Muenster cheese. Additional toppings may be added, such as onion, green peppers, olives, etc. Bake in 375 degree oven about 10 minutes.

Preparation time: 1 - 1 1/2 hours     Yield: 2-3 pizzas

Hint: This identical sauce (using ground beef, and with amounts multiplied) may be used for spaghetti, lasagna, and other Italian recipes. Any leftover pizza sauce may be frozen and saved for future Italian recipes.

Mrs. Vernon Dunn
St. Charles, Missouri

## MARY ANN PICKARD PIZZA "HOELSCHER STYLE"

**Pizza Crust:**

| | |
|---|---|
| 1 1/4 c. unbleached flour | 1 tsp. salt |
| 3/4 c. oat flour | 2/3 c. milk |
| 1 tsp. baking powder | 1/4 c. oil |

Stir together the flours, baking powder and salt in a mixing bowl. Pour the milk and oil into the flour mixture and stir until the dough holds together in a ball. Squeeze the dough with both hands several times, then pat and spread into a 14-inch round pizza pan. Bake at 425 degrees for 12-14 minutes.

**Pizza Topping:**

| | |
|---|---|
| 2 cans Chef-Boy-Ar-Dee's Pizza Sauce with cheese | 1 green pepper, chopped |
| 1 c. cooked ground beef or sausage | 1 c. sliced celery |
| 1 c. sliced carrots | 1 or 2 mushrooms, sliced |
| 1/2 medium onion, diced | 1/2 medium zucchini, sliced |
| | 3 Tbsp. oil |
| | 1 clove garlic, finely chopped |

Prepare vegetables; place oil and garlic in a heavy pan and saute vegetables until just tender. Cover pizza crust with sauce. Add meat, then vegetables. Top with cheese and bake at 425 degrees for 10-15 minutes.

Preparation time: 45 minutes          Yield: One 14-inch pizza

Hint: To make your own pizza sauce, combine one 15-ounce can tomato sauce, 1 tablespoon Italian seasoning, 1 teaspoon honey, 1 teaspoon salt, 1 teaspoon dried onion and 1/2 teaspoon oregano.

Carolyn Hoelscher
Ballwin, Missouri

## OVEN BEEF STEW

| | |
|---|---|
| 2 lb. beef stew meat, or any kind of beef roast, cut into bite-size pieces | 1 can onion soup |
| | 1 can cream of celery soup |
| | 4 c. cooked brown rice |

Put raw meat in a casserole. Stir the soups together (undiluted) and pour over the meat. Cover and bake in a 300 degree oven for 2 1/2 - 3 hours. Serve over the rice.

Preparation time: 3 hours          Yield: 6 servings

Betty Ritter
St. Marys, Missouri

# LASAGNE

| | |
|---|---|
| 1 lb. sausage | 3 eggs |
| 1/2 lb. hamburger | 3 c. cottage cheese |
| 1 clove garlic, minced | 3/4 c. grated Parmesan |
| 1 Tbsp. whole basil | 3 Tbsp. parsley flakes |
| 1 1/2 tsp. salt | 1/2 tsp. salt |
| 1 (1 lb.) can tomatoes | 3/4 tsp. pepper |
| 2 (6 oz.) cans tomato paste | 1/2 tsp. garlic salt |
| 12 oz. whole wheat lasagne noodles | 1 lb. Mozzarella cheese, shredded |

Brown meat and pour off all grease. Add next 5 ingredients and simmer, uncovered, for 35-40 minutes, stirring often. Cook lasagne noodles according to package directions. Drain and rinse with cold water. Drain thoroughly. Beat eggs and add remaining ingredients except the Mozzarella cheese.

Layer half the noodles in 13x9x2 inch baking dish. Spread with half the cottage cheese mixture and then half the Parmesan cheese. Then put on half of the meat sauce. Repeat and bake for 30 minutes at 375 degrees. Let stand 10-15 minutes to set before serving. Garnish with parsley.

Preparation time: 1 1/2 - 2 hours     Yield: 8-10 servings

Hint: This freezes nicely. I always make it up about 1 week before serving, thaw about 1 hour, then bake for 45 minutes.

Lou Sutton
Harrison, Arkansas


# BULGUR-GROUND BEEF CASSEROLE

| | |
|---|---|
| 1 lb. lean ground beef | 1/8 tsp. pepper |
| 2 stalks celery (1 c.), chopped | 1 (16 oz.) can tomatoes, cut up |
| 1 large green pepper, chopped | 1 c. bulgur wheat |
| 1 medium onion, chopped | 1 c. water |
| 1 clove garlic, minced | 1/2 c. raisins |
| 1 1/2 tsp. salt | 1/3 c. sunflower seeds |

In skillet cook beef, celery, green pepper, onion, garlic, salt and pepper until meat is brown and vegetables are crisp-tender. Drain off excess fat. Stir in undrained tomatoes, bulgur, water, raisins and sunflower seeds. Put in 2-quart casserole. Bake in 375 degree oven about 35 minutes. If desired, top with cheese during the last 5 minutes of baking.

Preparation time: 1 hour     Yield: 4-6 servings

Janet E. Griffin
Grand Junction, Colorado

## CUBAN FOOD

1 lb. lean ground beef
1 small onion
1/2 green pepper
Salt and pepper

2 Tbsp. capers
1/2 c. raisins
1 large can tomatoes
2 Tbsp. green olives

Brown meat and drain. Add remaining ingredients and simmer several hours. Serve over rice.

Preparation time: 3 - 3 1/2 hours    Yield: 4-6 servings

Jan Berryhill
Richmond, Virginia

## CHINESE MEAT DISH

2 large onions, chopped
3 Tbsp. butter or margarine
1 lb. ground beef
1 small can tomato soup (Hain)

4 oz. Cheddar cheese, cubed
2 c. cooked brown rice
Salt and pepper to taste

Brown onions in butter; add ground beef and brown. Stir in tomato soup and simmer for 20 minutes. Add cheese and stir the whole mixture into the rice; season with salt and pepper and bake at 300 degrees for 30 minutes.

Preparation time: 1 hour    Yield: 4-6 servings

## BEEF SURPRISE

1 Tbsp. oil, if desired
1/2 medium onion, chopped
1 green pepper, chopped
1 lb. ground beef

2 c. cooked whole wheat macaroni
6 slices Cheddar cheese
1 c. canned tomatoes
Salt and pepper

Saute onion and green pepper in oil until lightly browned; add ground beef and brown. Add cooked macaroni, cheese, and tomatoes. Stir until mixture has warmed throughout and cheese has melted; season to taste with salt and pepper.

Preparation time: 15 minutes    Yield: 4-6 servings

Betty Reynolds
Westville, Oklahoma

## ROMA MEAT LOAF

1 1/2 lb. ground beef
1 egg
1/2 c. finely chopped onion
3/4 c. wholegrain cracker
  crumbs
8 oz. tomato sauce

1 tsp. salt
1/2 tsp. oregano
1/8 tsp. pepper
2 c. shredded Mozzarella
  cheese

Mix all ingredients thoroughly, except for cheese and enough tomato sauce to spread on top of the loaf. Turn onto waxed paper or aluminum foil. Shape into a rectangle about 1 inch thick. Spread cheese over meat and roll meat (like a jelly roll). Seal ends and seam, then place in a loaf pan and bake 1 hour at 350 degrees. Pour off grease, add remaining tomato sauce, bake 15 minutes more.

Preparation time: 1 1/2 hours        Yield: 6-8 servings

Karen Reynolds
Siloam Springs, Arkansas

## NATURAL MEAT LOAF

1 1/2 c. ground beef
1/2 tsp. soy sauce
1 c. sunflower seed meal
1 egg
1 Tbsp. tomato juice

2 Tbsp. chopped onion
1 tsp. salt
1/2 c. powdered milk
1/2 c. milk

Mix ingredients lightly. Bake in an oiled pan at 350 degrees for about 1 hour. Serve with tomato sauce.

Preparation time: 1 hour        Yield: 6 servings
            15 minutes
Hint: I also make cabbage rolls from this recipe. Place cabbage leaves in pan of boiling water for 3 or 4 minutes, remove from pan. Place 2-3 tablespoons meat mixture in leaf, fold and place in pan. Pour additional tomato juice over rolls. Bake at 350 degrees for 45 minutes.

Lucille Willis
Mounds, Oklahoma

## ZUCCHINI AND BURGER CASSEROLE

4 c. thinly sliced zucchini
1 lb. lean ground beef
1/2 c. chopped onion
1 clove garlic, minced
1 c. cooked brown rice
1/2 c. tomato sauce

1/2 tsp. salt
1/2 tsp. dried oregano, crushed
1/4 tsp. pepper
1 beaten egg
1/2 c. cottage cheese
1/2 c. grated Cheddar (sharp) cheese

Cook zucchini in steamer until tender; drain well. In skillet cook ground beef, onion, and garlic together; drain when browned. Stir in rice, tomato sauce and spices. Combine egg, cottage cheese and cooked zucchini. Layer half of burger-rice mixture in 2-quart casserole dish. Add all cottage cheese-zucchini mixture. Add remaining burger mixture. Sprinkle cheese over top. Bake at 350 degrees for about 20-25 minutes.

Preparation time: 30-45 minutes    Yield: 6 servings

Diane McLean
Knoxville, Tennessee


## BARBECUED MEAT BALLS

1 lb. lean ground beef
  made into balls
1/2 onion, chopped
2 c. catsup (sweetened with
  honey)
1 c. water

2 tsp. Worcestershire sauce
  (optional)
2 Tbsp. honey
2 Tbsp. vinegar
Salt and pepper

Make meat balls, brown in skillet and drain. Bring remaining ingredients to a boil. Add meat balls and simmer for 45 minutes. Serve over spaghetti or rice. Can add cheese of choice; recipe can be doubled.

Preparation time: 1 hour    Yield: 4 generous servings

Mrs. Roy Fisher
Jonesboro, Arkansas

## HEARTY BEEF AND NOODLE CASSEROLE

1 lb. ground beef
1 Tbsp. oil
8 oz. frozen corn
3 tomatoes, cut up
8 oz. whole wheat noodles,
  cooked
1 c. grated Cheddar cheese
2 heaping Tbsp. protein
  (optional)

1/4 c. green olives
2 Tbsp. liquid from olives
1 small garlic
1 green pepper, diced (optional)
1 small onion, diced (optional)
1 tsp. salt
1/2 tsp. black pepper
1 1/2 tsp. chili powder

Brown beef in oil. Add corn, tomatoes, noodles, cheese, protein, and seasonings. Place remaining ingredients in blender, cover and process at "puree" until smooth. Add pureed mixture to meat mixture, mix lightly, and pour into greased 2-quart casserole dish. Cover and bake in preheated oven at 325 degrees for 45 minutes. Uncover and bake for an additional 10 minutes.

Preparation time: 1 hour          Yield: 6 servings
                10 minutes
    Hint: This recipe works fine without the extra protein if you prefer not to use it.

Diane Ruden
Marcus, Iowa


## PUERTO RICAN CASSEROLE

1 lb. hamburger or unseasoned
  ground pork or a
  combination of both
1 onion, cut in rings
15 black olives, halved
4 carrots, cleaned and cut
  into slices
2 stalks celery, sliced

1 (4 oz.) can mushroom stems
  and pieces plus juice
1/2 large green pepper, cut in
  chunks
1 tsp. dried sweet basil
1/2 tsp. cumin
1/2 tsp. garlic salt
4 tomatoes (fresh or canned)
3 strips bacon, cooked and
  broken into bits

Brown meat. Add fresh vegetables, except tomatoes; add spices and cook until vegetables are crisp-tender over medium-low heat. Add remaining ingredients and heat through. Serve over brown rice or whole-wheat spaghetti.

Preparation time: 45 minutes          Yield: 4 to 6 servings

Judy Beemer
Sharon Springs, Kansas

## HAMBURGER QUICHE

| | |
|---|---|
| 1/2 lb. lean ground beef | 3 green onions, chopped fine |
| 1/2 c. homemade mayonnaise | 8 oz. Cheddar cheese, cubed |
| 1/2 c. milk | Black pepper |
| 2 eggs | 9-inch pie shell, unbaked |
| 1 Tbsp. cornstarch | |

Preheat oven to 350 degrees; then brown meat and drain. Blend mayonnaise, milk, eggs, and cornstarch until smooth. Stir in remaining ingredients and turn into pie shell. Sprinkle mill grind black pepper over the top.
Bake 35-40 minutes or until knife inserted comes out clean.

Preparation time: 55 minutes        Yield: 1 quiche

Carol Ashberry
Cabot, Arkansas


## MEXICALI WHEAT SKILLET

| | |
|---|---|
| 1 lb. hamburger | 1/2 tsp. garlic powder |
| 1 c. chopped celery | Dash cayenne pepper |
| 1 c. chopped green pepper | 2 (1 lb.) cans tomatoes |
| 1 Tbsp. chili powder | 2 c. cooked wheat berries |
| 1 1/2 tsp. salt | |

Saute hamburger, celery and pepper in a large skillet until browned. Add chili powder, salt, garlic powder and cayenne pepper and stir well. Add remaining ingredients and simmer 15 minutes.

Preparation time: 30 minutes        Yield: 4-6 servings
Hint: To cook wheat berries, cover with lots of water and cook about 45 minutes; drain off excess water and use.

Rima Summers
Merritt Island, Florida

## MEXICAN CASSEROLE

1 lb. ground beef or
  pork sausage
2 Tbsp. oil
1/2 c. chopped onion
1 clove garlic, crushed
1 c. water
6 oz. tomato paste
4 oz. seeded chopped green
  chilies

1/4 c. salad olives, chopped
2 Tbsp. chili powder
1 c. grated Monterey Jack cheese
1 c. grated Cheddar cheese
1 (8 oz.) pkg. cream cheese,
  cut in 1/2 inch cubes
6 c. slightly crushed corn
  tortilla chips

Brown meat, onion, and garlic. Add remaining ingredients except cheeses and chips. Layer in order: 1/2 chips, 1/2 sauce, 1/2 cheese. Repeat. Bake at 350 degrees for 30-40 minutes or microwave for 12 minutes at 65% power.

Preparation time:
        50 minutes using oven
        25 minutes with microwave

Yield: 6-8 servings

Karen Shrum
Harrison, Arkansas


## SICILIAN SUPPER

1 lb. ground beef
1/2 c. chopped onion
6 oz. can tomato paste
3/4 c. water
1 1/2 tsp. salt
1/4 tsp. pepper

3/4 c. milk
8 oz. pkg. cream cheese
1/4 c. Parmesan cheese
1/2 tsp. garlic salt
1/2 c. chopped green pepper
2 c. whole wheat noodles, cooked

Brown meat and onions. Add tomato paste, water, salt and pepper; simmer 5 minutes. Heat milk and cream cheese. Blend well. Stir in 1/4 cup Parmesan cheese, garlic salt, green pepper and noodles to milk and cream cheese mixture. In 2-quart casserole dish, alternate layers of noodles and meat sauce. Bake at 350 degrees for 20 minutes. Sprinkle with Parmesan cheese.

Preparation time: 45 minutes

Yield: 6-8 servings

Karen Reynolds
Siloam Springs, Arkansas

## STUFFED SQUASH

1/2 c. brown rice, uncooked
1 lb. ground beef
1 can tomato sauce (15 1/2 oz.)
1 1/2 tsp. salad herbs
1 tsp. cinnamon

Salt and pepper
6 medium zucchini squash
2 Tbsp. chopped onion (optional)
Mint leaves (optional)

Combine rice, ground beef, 1/2 can tomato sauce, salad herbs, cinnamon and a sprinkling of salt and pepper. Slice washed zucchini lengthwise and scoop out to form a shell (saving pulp for later use). Stuff with meat mixture and arrange on a rack for steaming in a skillet. Steam zucchini in remaining tomato sauce mixed with 1/2 can of water; add chopped onion and mint leaves if desired. Cover and steam for 30-40 minutes adding water as necessary to keep from burning.

Preparation time: 1 hour          Yield: 4 to 6 servings
Hint: You may want to cook the rice for 15 minutes in 1 cup water, drain, then proceed as directed.

Catherine Kerr
Missouri City, Texas


## BEEF STUFFED EGGPLANT

2 small eggplants
1 lb. ground beef
1 large onion, chopped
1 c. fresh tomato with skin,
  chopped
2 Tbsp. olive oil
1/2 tsp. garlic juice
1 tsp. salt (or to taste)
1/2 c. wholegrain bread
  crumbs

1/2 tsp. pepper
2 tsp. oregano
2 tsp. Worcestershire sauce
  (optional)
1/4 c. chopped fresh parsley
  (optional)
1 c. water
1 1/2 c. Cheddar cheese, grated
Grated Parmesan cheese

Wash eggplant, and cut in half lengthwise. Remove pulp, leaving a 1/4-inch shell; set aside. Cut pulp into small cubes. Saute pulp, ground beef, onion and tomato in oil until beef is browned. Stir in garlic juice, salt, pepper, oregano, Worcestershire sauce and parsley (if desired). Mix in the bread crumbs and stuff the eggplant shells. Place in a 13x9x2-inch baking dish. add the 1 cup water in the bottom of the dish. Cover tightly with aluminum foil and bake at 375 degrees for 20-25 minutes. Remove foil and top each eggplant half with grated Cheddar cheese. Sprinkle with Parmesan cheese and bake an additional 5 minutes or until cheese melts.

Preparation time: 50-60 minutes     Yield: 4 servings

Mrs. Carl F. Maples, Sr.
Knoxville, Tennessee

## SAUSAGE SOUFFLE

1 lb. sausage
6 slices wholegrain bread
  (with crusts trimmed)
4 eggs

2 c. milk
1/4 c. grated Cheddar cheese
1 tsp. dry mustard
Salt to taste

Brown and drain sausage. Cube bread and place in buttered casserole. Cover with sausage. Beat eggs, milk, cheese, dry mustard and salt. Pour over bread. Cover with foil and refrigerate overnight. Remove foil and bake at 350 degrees for 45 minutes. Reduce to 325 degrees and bake 15 minutes longer.

Preparation time: 15 minutes +
     overnight + baking time

Yield: 6 servings

Jean Myers
Joplin, Missouri

## SCALLOPED HAM AND CABBAGE

1 1/2 c. cubed cooked ham
1 1/2 c. grated Cheddar cheese,
  (save 3/4 c. for topping)
1 1/2 c. thick white sauce

3 Tbsp. chopped onion
3 Tbsp. chopped parsley
1 qt. cooked, drained cabbage
  (barely done)

Mix all ingredients. Sprinkle cheese on top. Bake at 400 degrees for about 45 minutes, until brown on top.

Hint: To make a thick white sauce, melt 6 tablespoons butter or margarine in a heavy skillet. Add 6 tablespoons wholegrain flour and cook, stirring constantly, until bubbly. Add 1 1/2 cups milk all at once, stirring with a wire whisk constantly as you add. Continue cooking and stirring until bubbly and thickened. Season as desired.

Nona Rogero
Jacksonville, Florida

DESSERTS

# PEANUT BUTTER CUPCAKES

1/4 c. natural style peanut
   butter
1/4 c. softened butter
1/4 c. honey
1/2 c. maple syrup
1 egg

1/4 tsp. salt
1/2 tsp. vanilla
1 c. whole wheat flour or
   3/4 c. unbleached flour
1 1/4 tsp. baking powder
3/8 c. milk

Cream peanut butter and butter until smooth. Beat in honey, maple syrup, egg, salt and vanilla. Sift flour and baking powder, and add alternately with milk. Fill paper lined muffin tins half full and bake for 20 minutes at 375 degrees.

Preparation time: 25 minutes     Yield: 12 cupcakes

**Frosting:**

1/2 c. natural style peanut
   butter

2 tsp. butter
2 tsp. honey

Beat thoroughly and smooth onto cooled cupcakes.

Hint: If frosting seems too stiff, add more butter and honey in equal amounts.

Jackie Kelsey
Mt. Carmel, Illinois


# ITALIAN APPLE CAKE

1/2 c. honey
4 apples, quartered and
   sliced thin
2 tsp. cinnamon
2 c. unbleached flour
1 c. date sugar

1 1/2 tsp. soda
Pinch salt
3 eggs
3/4 c. softened butter
1/2 fresh lemon, squeezed

Combine honey, apples, and cinnamon; set aside. Measure flour, date sugar, soda and salt; set aside. Beat eggs and add butter and lemon juice, then the flour mixture. Fold in the apple mixture, place in an oiled 7x11-inch or shallow 2-quart pan, and bake at 350 degrees for 40 minutes.

Preparation time: 1 hour     Yield: 1 cake

Judy Aversa
Fontana, California

# CHERRY CAKE PUDDING

1/4 c. butter, melted
  in 9x9-inch pan
1 1/4 c. whole wheat flour
3/4 c. fructose

2 1/2 tsp. baking powder
1 c. milk
1 can tart cherries, drained
2 Tbsp. fructose

Mix dry ingredients together and pour over melted butter. Sweeten the cherries with the 2 tablespoons fructose, and spoon over the batter. Bake 45 minutes at 325 degrees.

Preparation time: 55 minutes          Yield: 9 servings

Larraine Etnier
Collins, Iowa

# SUPER MOIST CAROB CAKE

1 c. whole wheat flour
1 c. unbleached flour
1/2 c. fructose
2 sticks (1 c.) butter or
  margarine
4 Tbsp. carob powder

1 c. honey
1/2 c. water
1 tsp. soda
1/2 c. buttermilk
2 beaten eggs
1 tsp. vanilla

Mix together flours and fructose; set aside. Combine butter, carob powder, honey, and water in a saucepan and heat to boiling but do not boil. Pour the hot mixture over the flour mixture and beat until well blended. Dissolve soda in buttermilk and add to the batter along with the beaten eggs and vanilla. Mix well about 2 minutes with an electric mixer. Pour into well-oiled pans either one 9x13-inch or two 8-inch round layer pans. Bake 40-45 minutes at 350 degrees.

Preparation time: 1 hour          Yield: 1 sheet or 2 layers

### Frosting:

1 1/2 c. fructose
1/3 c. water
2 egg whites

1/4 tsp. cream of tartar
1 tsp. vanilla

Heat fructose in water until it dissolves. Slowly pour the hot mixture over the egg whites and cream of tartar while beating with an electric mixer on high speed. Continue beating for 7 minutes, adding vanilla at the end of the beating time. Refrigerate after frosting.

Preparation time: 10 minutes          Yield: Frosting for a sheet or
                                            2 layer cake

Cheryl Patrick
Harrison, Arkansas

# CAROB CAKE

1/2 c. butter or margarine
1 c. honey
1 egg
2 c. whole wheat flour
1/3 c. carob

1 tsp. soda
1/2 tsp. cinnamon
1/8 tsp. salt
3/4 c. hot water
1/2 c. chopped nuts

Cream butter and honey, fold in egg and beat. In another bowl, sift flour, carob, soda, cinnamon, and salt. Add dry ingredients alternately with hot water. Stir in nuts if desired, then whip mixture until almost fluffy. Pour into a lightly greased 9x9-inch pan and bake 1 hour at 250 degrees or until cake is moist and shrinks away from pan. Eat as brownies or frost with Carob Frosting. (below)

Preparation time: 1 1/2 hours        Yield: 1 square cake

### Carob Frosting:

1/4 c. honey
2 Tbsp. butter or margarine
2/3 c. powdered milk

1/3 c. carob powder
3 Tbsp. cream
1 tsp. vanilla

Cream honey and butter, add milk and carob powder; blend. Beat in cream and vanilla and whip until smooth and creamy.

Preparation time: 10 minutes        Yield: Frosting for 1 layer cake
Hint: Recipe may be doubled or tripled for a 2 or 3 layer cake.

Linda Campbell
Carlton, Texas


# CRANBERRY CAKE

2 1/2 c. unbleached flour
1/2 c. whole wheat flour
2 tsp. baking powder
1 tsp. soda
1 tsp. cinnamon
1/2 tsp. cloves

1/2 tsp. salt
3 carrots, scraped and
   cut into chunks
1 c. whole cranberry sauce
1 1/2 - 2 c. honey
4 eggs

Combine dry ingredients, then set aside. Place carrots, cranberries, honey and eggs in blender and chop. Add to dry ingredients, mix well, and place in 2 greased 9x5-inch loaf pans. Bake at 325 degrees for one hour.

Preparation time: 1 1/2 hours        Yield: 2 loaves
Hint: To make cranberry sauce, combine 8 ounces washed cranberries, 1/2 cup fructose and 1 cup boiling water. Cook 10 minutes, skim off froth and cool. Use 1 cup prepared sauce in cake.

Jackie Buxton
Harrison, Arkansas

# CAROB BROWNIE CAKE

2 c. whole wheat or whole
  wheat pastry flour
1/2 c. butter
4 Tbsp. carob powder
1 c. water
1 tsp. vanilla

1/2 tsp. salt
1/3 - 1/2 c. honey
1/2 c. sour milk or 1/2 c.
  sweet milk + 1 Tbsp. vinegar
1 tsp. soda
2 eggs, beaten

Place flour in bowl. Bring to boil: butter, carob powder, water, vanilla and salt. Add to flour, together with honey. Beat well. Beat soda into sour milk. Add to mixture with beaten eggs. Put into a 17x11x3/4-inch greased and floured cookie sheet and bake at 325 degrees to 350 degrees for 20 minutes. Ice while hot with icing below.

Preparation time: 30 minutes    Yield: 1 cake

### Carob Icing:

2 Tbsp. carob powder
1/2 c. butter
1 tsp. vanilla
1/3 c. honey

1/2 c. powdered milk
2-3 tsp. milk (more if necessary
  for consistency)
1/2 - 1 c. chopped nuts

Beat ingredients together until creamy, about 5 minutes.

Preparation time: 5 minutes    Yield: Frosting for above cake

Kathleen Hackman
London, Arkansas

# HONEY OF A CAKE

1 c. oats
1/2 c. butter
1 1/2 c. boiling water
3/4 - 1 c. honey
1 tsp. vanilla
2 eggs

1 3/4 c. whole wheat flour
1 tsp. soda
3/4 tsp. salt
1 tsp. cinnamon
1/4 tsp. nutmeg
1/2 - 1 c. chopped nuts
Raisins and apples (optional)

Put oats, butter and boiling water in large bowl and let set 20 minutes. Add honey, vanilla and eggs and mix well. Add rest of ingredients which have been stirred together. Mix well and pour into 13x9-inch pan which has been greased and floured. Bake at 350 degrees for 30-40 minutes. Ice with honey butter mixture—1/2 honey and 1/2 butter.

Preparation time: 1 hour    Yield: One 13x9-inch cake

Kathleen Hackman
London, Arkansas

## BOILED MAPLE CAKE

1 c. maple syrup
1/2 c. melted butter or
 margarine
1 tsp. cloves
1 tsp. nutmeg
1 tsp. cinnamon

1 tsp. salt
1 c. seedless raisins
1 c. cold water
2 c. unbleached flour
1 tsp. soda
1/2 c. chopped nuts (optional)

Boil first 8 ingredients together for 4 minutes. Chill thoroughly, then add remaining ingredients. Beat well and bake in greased loaf pan at 350 degrees for 1 hour. Good plain, but add Boiled Maple Frosting for special occasions.

Preparation time: 2 hours          Yield: 1 cake

### Boiled Maple Frosting:

**1 egg white**                    **1 c. maple syrup**

Place the egg white in a mixing bowl. Boil the syrup to the soft ball stage (238 degrees on the candy thermometer). Remove from heat. Beat the egg white quickly until stiff. Pour the hot syrup in a fine stream over the white, beating constantly. Continue beating until mixture is stiff enough to spread. This makes enough for the maple cake, but recipe can easily be doubled for a layer cake.

Preparation time: 20 minutes       Yield: Frosting for a one layer cake

Sara Tatham
Plymouth, New Hampshire

## BANANA CAKE

1/2 c. butter or margarine
2/3 c. fructose
1 c. mashed ripe banana
2 eggs
1 tsp. vanilla

1 c. oat flour
3/4 c. unbleached flour
1 tsp. soda
1/2 c. chopped nuts

Topping:

3/4 c. rolled oats
1/4 c. honey
2 Tbsp. melted butter

2 Tbsp. chopped nuts
1/2 tsp. cinnamon

Cream together butter and fructose; blend in mashed banana, eggs and vanilla. Combine dry ingredients and gradually add to creamed mixture, stirring well after each addition. Stir in nuts and pour into greased 8x8-inch baking pan. Mix topping ingredients together and sprinkle topping on. Bake in preheated oven at 350 degrees for 40-45 minutes.

Preparation time: 1 hour          Yield: 1 square cake
Hint: To cook in microwave, change rolled oats in topping to 1 cup, use glass baking dish. Microwave on high for 3 minutes, rotate, and bake 3 minutes more, checking for doneness.

Lona Yender
Nemaha, Iowa

## HONEY OATMEAL CAKE

1 c. oats
1 stick butter
1 1/4 c. boiling water
1 1/2 c. honey
1 tsp. vanilla
2 eggs

1 3/4 c. sifted whole wheat flour
1 tsp. soda
3/4 tsp. salt
1 tsp. cinnamon
1/4 tsp. nutmeg

Put oats, butter, and boiling water in large bowl and let set for 20 minutes. Add honey, vanilla and eggs. Add rest of ingredients and pour into greased and floured 9x13-inch pan. Bake 30-40 minutes at 350 degrees.

Preparation time: 1 hour          Yield: 24 servings
                    10 minutes
Hint: You may want to decrease the honey to 1 cup depending on your personal preference.

Debi Thullen
Berkley, Michigan

# CHEESECAKE SUPREME

1 c. unbleached flour
1/4 c. fructose
1 tsp. lemon juice
1/2 c. butter or margarine
1 egg yolk, slightly beaten
  (save white for filling)
1/4 tsp. vanilla
5 (8 oz.) pkg. cream cheese

1/4 tsp. vanilla
1 tsp. lemon juice
1 1/2 c. honey
3 Tbsp. unbleached flour
1/4 tsp. salt
5 eggs
1/4 c. whipping cream

Combine first 3 ingredients, then cut in butter until mixture is crumbly. Add egg yolk and vanilla; blend thoroughly. Pat 1/3 of dough onto bottom of a 9-inch springform pan, (sides removed). Bake in a 400 degree oven about 8 minutes or until golden; cool. Attach sides to bottom, lightly buttering sides before the remaining dough is patted onto the sides of the pan to a height of 2 inches.

Soften cream cheese and beat until creamy, adding vanilla and lemon juice, then honey. Add the eggs, one at a time, beating lightly after each addition. Add the egg white which was left from the crust, beating just to blend. Gently stir in cream. Pour cheese mixture carefully into the crust-lined springform pan and bake at 450 degrees for 12 minutes. Reduce heat to 300 degrees and continue baking for 55-60 minutes. Remove from oven and cool for 30 minutes. Loosen sides with spatula, cool 30 more minutes, then remove sides. Allow to cool an additional 2 hours, then top with glaze.

**Glaze:**

3 Tbsp. fructose
1 Tbsp. cornstarch
1 large can unsweetened
  pineapple with juice

1/2 tsp. lemon juice
3/4 c. whipping cream
1 tsp. fructose

Combine fructose and cornstarch in saucepan; stir in 1 cup pineapple juice and lemon juice. Heat, stirring constantly, until mixture comes to a boil. Cook and stir until thick and clear. Cool to room temperature. Spread drained, crushed pineapple on cheesecake. Cover with glaze. Let cool completely and cover with whipped cream sweetened with fructose. Chill at least 2 hours or until very cold.

Preparation time: 5-6 hours (total)    Yield: 1 large cheesecake

Marie Raney
Dogpatch, Arkansas

## PINEAPPLE SUPREME CAKE

1 c. honey
1/4 c. fructose
2 eggs
1 (13 oz.) can unsweetened
  crushed pineapple
  (do not drain)
1 3/4 c. unbleached flour or
  whole wheat flour

1 tsp. salt
2 tsp. soda
1 c. chopped nuts (or part
  unsweetened coconut)
1 tsp. vanilla

Mix first 4 ingredients in medium bowl; set aside. Mix dry ingredients and add only until well blended; adding vanilla last. Bake in a well-greased and floured 9x13-inch pan for 30-40 minutes at 350 degrees. When cake is almost finished baking, make topping; cool slightly, prick thoroughly with toothpick, and pour topping slowly over warm cake.

**Topping:**

3/4 c. butter
1/2 c. + 1 Tbsp. fructose

1/2 c. evaporated milk
1 tsp. vanilla

Bring to a boil and cook 4 minutes, being careful not to scorch. Proceed as directed above.

Preparation time: 1 1/2 hours       Yield: One 9x13-inch cake

Janet Campbell
Corvallis, Oregon

## CREAM CHEESE FROSTING

1 (8 oz.) pkg. cream cheese,
  softened
1-2 Tbsp. butter, softened

Milk (small amount)
Honey

Drizzle in honey while beating until fluffy and to your taste. Good on zucchini bars or brownies.

Preparation time: 5 minutes       Yield: 1 1/4 cups

Kathy Ortmann
Marcus, Iowa

# BLACKBERRY CREAM PIE

| | |
|---|---|
| 1 1/2 c. crunchy granola | 12 oz. cream cheese |
| 3/4 c. Nutrigrain cereal™ | 1/3 c. fructose |
| 3 Tbsp. butter | 1/2 c. boiling water |
| 2 c. blackberries (fresh | 1 pkg. unflavored gelatin |
|   or frozen) | 1 tsp. vanilla |

Place granola and Nutrigrain™ cereal in blender and process until mixture has the texture of crumbs throughout. Put crumbs in 9-inch pie pan and add the melted butter. Stir until all crumbs have been moistened, then pat into a pie shell. Bake for 7 minutes at 350 degrees. Place blackberries in food processor or blender and puree. Add cream cheese and fructose and blend until mixture is thoroughly mixed. Dissolve unflavored gelatin in boiling water and add to the above mixture. Blend once again. Add vanilla, stir and pour into pie shell. Freeze pie for 2 hours and then refrigerate. Serve cold.

Preparation time: 20 minutes +  Yield: One 9-inch pie
               freezing time         6-8 servings
    Hint: If you don't have Nutrigrain™ cereal, use 2 1/4 cups crunchy granola for crust. Also, this is even more delicious the second day.

Lou Ann Daugherty
Siloam Springs, Arkansas


# HONEY APPLE PIE

| | |
|---|---|
| 4-6 large apples (peeled | 2 Tbsp. lemon juice |
|   cored and sliced thin) | 1/2 c. honey |
| 1/4 c. water | 1 tsp. cinnamon |
| 3 Tbsp. cornstarch (heaping) | 1/2 tsp. almond |
| 2 Tbsp. honey | Crust for 2-crust 9-inch pie |

Slowly cook apples and water. Meanwhile, mix cornstarch, 2 table-spoons honey, and lemon juice; add to apples when almost cooked along with honey, cinnamon and almond. Pour mixture into pie shell, adjust top crust with steam vents and bake in oven at 425 degrees for 10 minutes or until nicely browned.

Preparation time: 30 minutes  Yield: 1 pie

Ruth Ann Peters
Harrison, Arkansas

# CHERRY PIE

Crust for 9-inch 2-crust pie
4 c. red sour cherries
3 Tbsp. tapioca

1/2 tsp. almond extract
1 1/3 c. honey (very light and mild)
Butter

Prepare pie crust then mix cherries, tapioca, almond extract and honey. Pour into pie shell and dot with butter. Adjust top crust with steam vents, then bake at 400 degrees for 15 minutes, reduce oven temperature to 350 degrees and finish baking until fruit is tender, about 20 minutes.

Preparation time: 1 hour          Yield: One 9-inch pie
    Hint: Be sure to bake the pie on a cookie sheet as it will probably boil over.

Janet Shumaker
Delta, Ohio


# CHEESECAKE PIE

2 monster granola cookies
  (made by Healthway)
1 1/2 tsp. cinnamon
3 Tbsp. butter or margarine,
  melted
1 (8 oz.) pkg. cream cheese
1/4 c. honey
1 egg
1 tsp. lemon juice
1/2 tsp. vanilla

1 c. sour cream
1 Tbsp. honey
1/2 tsp. vanilla
1/2 c. honey, warmed
1/2 c. unsweetened cherry juice
3 Tbsp. cornstarch
1/2 Tbsp. butter or margarine
1/8 c. lemon juice
1/4 tsp. almond flavoring
1 can sour red cherries

Make a crumb crust with blended cookie crumbs, cinnamon, and butter; press into a 9-inch pie pan. Mix cream cheese, 1/4 cup honey, egg, 1 teaspoon lemon juice and 1/2 teaspoon vanilla until smooth and pour into pie pan; bake at 350 degrees for 25 minutes. Blend sour cream with 1 tablespoon honey and 1/2 teaspoon vanilla; spread over slightly cooled cake and bake at 350 degrees for 15 minutes. Meanwhile, combine honey, cherry juice and cornstarch, mixing thoroughly to blend. Cook over medium heat, stirring until thick. Add butter, lemon juice and almond flavoring, then stir in cherries. Cool, then spread over cooled pie and chill.

Preparation time: 1 1/2 hours          Yield: 1 pie

Catherine Kerr
Missouri City, Texas

# GOLDEN CARROT PIE

2 c. sliced cooked carrots,
  pureed
3 eggs, slightly beaten
1/2 tsp. salt
1/2 tsp. ginger
1/2 tsp. nutmeg

1 tsp. cinnamon
1/8 tsp. cloves
3/4 c. evaporated milk
1 c. honey
1 unbaked 9-inch pie shell

Combine carrots, eggs, salt and spices, mix well. Add milk and honey, blending well (until smooth). Pour filling into pie shell. Bake at 400 degrees for 40-45 minutes. Allow pie to cool. May be garnished with whipped cream before serving.

Preparation time: 1 hour
              15 minutes

Yield: One 9-inch pie

Virginia McWilliams
Atlanta, Texas


# BUTTERNUT SQUASH PIE

2 c. cooked, mashed butternut
  squash
3/4 c. honey
2 eggs, beaten
1/4 c. milk

1/4 c. melted butter or margarine
1 tsp. cinnamon
1 tsp. allspice
1 unbaked 9-inch pie shell

Combine squash, honey, eggs, milk and butter, beating until mixed thoroughly. Blend in spices, then pour into pie shell and bake at 400 degrees for 40-50 minutes. Pie is done when a knife inserted in the center comes out clean. Cool and serve.

Preparation time: 1 hour
Yield: One 9-inch pie

Hint: To cook butternut squash, wash, quarter and seed. Cover with water and boil gently until tender. Scoop out pulp and proceed as directed.

Sue Rouse
Mobile, Alabama

## SWEET POTATO PIE

1 1/2 c. sweet potatoes, mashed
1/2 stick butter, softened
2 Tbsp. honey
1 c. evaporated milk

2 slightly beaten eggs
1 c. fructose
3 Tbsp. unbleached flour
1 (9-inch) baked pie crust

Mix first 5 ingredients with mixer until well blended. Add fructose and flour and mix for 2 minutes. Pour into a lightly browned pie crust. Bake at 350 degrees for 40-45 minutes until knife comes out clean.

Preparation time: 1 hour          Yield: One 9-inch pie

Mrs. Kathy Horton
Ocean Springs, Mississippi


## SHREDDED WHEAT PIE CRUST

3 large shredded wheat
  biscuits
1 Tbsp. honey

3 Tbsp. butter or margarine
  (softened or melted)

Crush cereal to make 1 cup tiny pieces. Using fingers, mix honey and butter with the crushed cereal. Press mixture onto bottom and sides of a 9-inch pie plate. Bake at 400 degrees for 5 minutes; turn off oven and leave crust in oven for 5 minutes longer. Remove from oven and let cool before filling as desired.

Preparation time: 20 minutes          Yield: One 9-inch pie crust

Sara Tatham
Plymouth, New Hampshire


## JANET'S PIE CRUST

1 3/4 c. unbleached flour
1/2 - 1 tsp. salt

1/2 c. oil
1/4 c. milk

Mix together and chill in refrigerator. Roll out on waxed paper. Will never fail.

Preparation time: 15 minutes          Yield: 2 crusts

Janet Shumaker
Delta, Ohio

## WHOLE WHEAT PIE CRUST

2 c. whole wheat flour
1/2 c + 2 tsp. oil

1 tsp. salt
1/4 c. cold milk

Mix together all ingredients and roll between wax paper. Peel off top wax paper and lay upside down pie plate on dough and wax paper. Flip everything over and peel off second wax paper from dough. Dough will gently fall into pie plate. Can fill unbaked crust and cover with second crust or bake two pie crusts. Bake at 425 degrees for 8 minutes.

Preparation time: 15 minutes          Yield: Two 9-inch pie crusts

Ruth Ann Peters
Harrison, Arkansas


## WHOLE WHEAT CRUST #2

1 1/2 c. unsifted unbleached
    flour
1 c. unsifted whole wheat
    flour (or you may use all
    whole wheat)

2 Tbsp. wheat germ
3/4 tsp. salt
1/2 c. oil
1/2 c. boiling water

Stir together flours, wheat germ and salt. Stir in oil and water. Mix until all is moistened, then gather into a ball. Divide in half; roll out between waxed paper.

Preparation time: 10-15 minutes          Yield: Double crust for 10-inch pie

Janet Griffin
Grand Junction, Colorado


## CAROB CHIP COOKIES

1/2 c. butter, softened
1 c. honey
2 eggs, slightly beaten
2 1/4 c. unbleached flour
2 tsp. baking powder

1 tsp. salt
1 c. nuts
1 tsp. vanilla
1 pkg. unsweetened carob chips

In a large bowl, cream butter and honey. Add eggs. Add flour, baking powder, salt, nuts, vanilla and carob chips. Mix well. Chill dough. Drop by teaspoonfuls on oiled cookie sheet. Bake at 350 degrees for 10-12 minutes.

Preparation time: 45 minutes          Yield: 4-5 dozen

Carole Shearer
Harrison, Arkansas

## PEANUT BUTTER DROP COOKIES

1 c. natural peanut butter
1/2 c. soft butter
2 tsp. vanilla
1/4 c. fructose
1 c. honey

2 eggs
2 1/2 c. unbleached flour
1 tsp. soda
1 c. coarsely chopped dry
    roasted peanuts

Put first six ingredients in bowl and beat together thoroughly. Combine flour and soda and slowly beat into above mixture. Stir peanuts in by hand. Drop by teaspoon onto greased cookie sheet and bake in a 375 degree oven for about 10 minutes, watching carefully.

Preparation time: 10 minutes +          Yield: 8 dozen
                    baking time
    Hint: Cookie dough may also be shaped into a roll, chilled or frozen, then sliced and baked. Be careful not to overbake—slightly underbaking produces a chewier cookie.

Genevieve Russell
Dallas, Texas


## NATURAL COOKIES

1/2 c. oil
2 c. natural style peanut
    butter
2 c. honey
2 eggs
2 tsp. vanilla
3 1/2 c. whole wheat flour
1 1/2 tsp. baking powder

1 tsp. cinnamon
3/4 c. raw wheat germ
4 c. oats
3/4 c. chopped nuts (or omit if
    you use crunchy peanut
    butter)
1 c. raisins

Mix oil, peanut butter, honey, eggs and vanilla thoroughly. Add flour, baking powder and cinnamon and mix well. Stir in wheat germ, oats, nuts and raisins. Shape into saucer size cookies; bake at 300 degrees for 15 minutes or until done.

Preparation time: 25-30 minutes     Yield: About 18 large cookies
    Hint: You may need to moisten hands with water to shape cookies.

Judy Harned
Coyle, Oklahoma

# HONEY-CAROB CHIP COOKIES

3 c. whole wheat flour
1/2 c. wheat germ
2 tsp. baking powder
1 tsp. soda
1 tsp. salt

2 c. natural style peanut butter
1 1/2 c. honey
2 eggs, beaten
2 tsp. vanilla
6 oz. unsweetened carob chips

Mix together dry ingredients and set aside. Cream together peanut butter and honey; add eggs and vanilla and mix thoroughly. Add half the dry ingredients, beat thoroughly; add remaining dry ingredients and blend, mixing by hand if necessary. Lightly oil hands and roll mixture into balls. Place on oiled cookie sheet and crisscross with fork. Bake for 10-12 minutes at 350 degrees.

Preparation time: 45 minutes          Yield: 4-5 dozen large cookies
Hint: Dip fork in cold water to prevent sticking; also, it is helpful to warm the peanut butter and honey before it is blended with the other ingredients.

Sherry Twigg
Milan, New Mexico

# NATURAL TOLLHOUSE COOKIES
# OR CAROB CHIP COOKIES

1 c. soft butter
3/4 c. honey
1 tsp. vanilla
1-2 tsp. water
2 eggs

2 1/4 c. whole wheat flour
1 tsp. soda
1 tsp. salt
2 c. unsweetened carob chips
1 c. nuts, if desired

Cream together butter, honey, vanilla, water and eggs. Add flour, soda and salt. Mix thoroughly. Stir in carob chips and nuts. Spoon onto lightly greased cookie sheet, (use safflower oil to grease). Bake at 350 degrees for 8-10 minutes.

Preparation time: 1 hour          Yield: 60-75 average size cookies,
                                          80-100 small size cookies

Cathy Bodell
Fullerton, California

## CAROB CHIP COOKIES

2 1/2 c. unbleached flour
1 tsp. soda
1 tsp. salt
1 c. softened butter or
  margarine

3/4 c. honey
1/2 c. fructose
1 tsp. vanilla
1 large or 2 small eggs
6 oz. pkg. unsweetened carob chips

Mix together dry ingredients; set aside. Beat butter, honey, fructose, and vanilla thoroughly; add egg and beat well. Add flour mixture, then carob chips. Roll into balls and bake on cookie sheets at 375 degrees for 10 minutes being careful not to overcook.

Preparation time: 15 minutes +
                baking time

Yield: 100 cookies

Cheryl Patrick
Harrison, Arkansas


## NUTRITIONAL OATMEAL DROP COOKIES

1/2 c. oat flour
1/2 c. whole wheat pastry
  flour
2 Tbsp. soy flour
1/4 c. powdered milk
1/4 tsp. salt
1/4 c. fructose
1/2 c. oil
1/2 c. honey

2 eggs, beaten
1 tsp. vanilla
1 c. rolled oats
1/4 c. wheat germ
1/2 c. unprocessed bran
3/4 c. walnuts (optional)
1/2 c. chopped dates (optional)
1 - 1 1/2 c. unsweetened coconut
  (optional)
1/2 c. unsweetened carob chips
  (optional)

Blend flours, powdered milk, and salt. Add fructose to the oil, honey, eggs and vanilla, then add the wet ingredients to the flour mixture. Blend thoroughly, then mix in the oats, wheat germ, bran, and optional ingredients as desired. Drop onto oiled sheets and bake for 12 minutes at 325 degrees.

Preparation time: 15 minutes +
                baking time

Yield: 2 1/2 - 3 dozen

Larraine Etnier
Collins, Iowa

# BIG BATCH OATMEAL RAISIN COOKIES

6 heaping c. oats
1 3/4 - 2 c. unbleached flour
1/2 c. wheat germ
1/2 tsp. salt
2 c. honey
2 c. butter (or 1 c. butter and
  1 c. margarine)

2 tsp. vanilla
2 tsp. soda dissolved in
  1 c. boiling water
2-3 c. raisins
1/2 - 1 c. broken walnuts

Mix oats, flour, wheat germ and salt. Cream honey, butter and vanilla and add to oat mixture. Add soda dissolved in water; beat well. Stir in raisins and nuts and drop by teaspoonfuls onto oiled cookie sheet. Bake at 350 degrees for 10 minutes.

Preparation time: 1 1/2 hours          Yield: 100 cookies
    Hint: Soften raisins by covering with hot water for 10 minutes; drain and add to cookies. Save water to lightly sweeten tea.

Marsha Hills
Peace River, Alberta, Canada


# SOFT GINGER COOKIES

1 c. butter or margarine
1/2 c. fructose
1 egg
1/2 c. dark honey
1 Tbsp. lemon juice
3/4 c. evaporated milk
3 c. sifted unbleached flour

1 tsp. soda
1/2 tsp. salt
1/2 tsp. ginger
1/2 tsp. cinnamon
1 (6 oz.) pkg. carob chips
1/2 c. chopped walnuts

Cream butter. Add fructose, and cream thoroughly. Add egg and honey; blend well. Stir lemon juice into evaporated milk; add to creamed mixture. Sift dry ingredients together. Add to creamed mixture and blend. Stir in chips and nuts. Drop by tablespoonfuls, 2 inches apart, on greased cookie sheet. Bake at 375 degrees for 10-12 minutes. Store in covered container.

Preparation time: 30 minutes          Yield: 4-5 dozen cookies
    Hint: I added the bran from the flour (after sifting) and included it in the dough.

Carol Mehegan
West Plains, Missouri

# BEEHIVES

1/4 c. honey
1 egg, beaten
1 tsp. vanilla
2 c. shredded unsweetened coconut

1 c. coarsely chopped walnuts
1 c. chopped dates
2 Tbsp. unbleached flour

In mixing bowl, combine honey, egg and vanilla. Beat until well blended. Stir in coconut and nuts. Shake dates in a bag with 2 tablespoons flour; add to mixture. Drop by tablespoonfuls onto a greased cookie sheet. Bake at 350 degrees for 12 minutes or until done.

Preparation time: 30 minutes          Yield: 2 1/2 dozen

Judy M. Aversa
Fontana, California

# 14 CARAT COOKIES

1/2 c. raisins
1/2 c. boiling water
1 c. whole wheat flour
1 3/4 tsp. baking powder
1 tsp. cinnamon
1/2 tsp. each: nutmeg, mace,
   allspice and cloves

1 tsp. vanilla
1/2 tsp. salt
1/2 tsp. soda
1/2 c. honey
1/2 c. oil
1 egg
1 c. grated carrots
1 tsp. lemon extract

Soak raisins in boiling water for 5 minutes. Mix dry ingredients in a bowl, then mix honey, oil, egg, carrots and lemon; add raisins. Blend all ingredients together, then drop by teaspoonfuls onto oiled cookie sheets and bake at 350 degrees for 8-12 minutes.

Preparation time: 30 minutes          Yield: 40 cookies
   Hint: These are mild tasting cookies, perfect for small children.

# HONEY CHEWS

1 c. honey
1 c. oil
1 tsp. vanilla
1 c. oats

1 c. unsweetened coconut
1/2 tsp. salt
1 c. soy flour
2 c. whole wheat flour

Combine first 6 ingredients. Mix well. Add flour one cup at a time and mix well. Drop by teaspoon on greased cookie sheet. Bake at 350 degrees until browned.

Preparation time: 45 minutes          Yield: 4-5 dozen

Janet Hillstrand
Harlan, Iowa

## CRISP HONEY COOKIES

1/2 c. butter
1/2 c. honey
1 3/4 c. unbleached flour
1 tsp. soda

1/2 tsp. cinnamon
1/4 tsp. cloves
1/3 c. wheat germ

Cream butter and honey. Sift together flour, soda and spices and mix in wheat germ. Combine dry ingredients with creamed mixture. Chill about one hour. Roll on lightly floured board to about 1/8 inch thickness and cut out as desired. Bake on greased cookie sheet at 350 degrees for 8-10 minutes.

Preparation time: 1 1/2 hours      Yield: 4-5 dozen
   (counting chilling time)

Carole Shearer
Harrison, Arkansas


## HEALTH COOKIES

1 1/4 c. oil
1/2 c. butter or margarine
1/2 c. honey
6 bananas
6 eggs
3 tsp. vanilla
6 c. whole wheat flour
2 1/2 c. oats
1 qt. pkg. powdered milk
1 1/2 tsp. salt

1 1/2 tsp. soda
1 tsp. baking powder
1 Tbsp. cinnamon
1 tsp. cloves
1 c. chopped nuts
2 c. raisins
1 c. unsweetened coconut, or
   3 c. raw shredded apple, or
   1-2 c. unsweetened applesauce

Cream oil, butter, honey, bananas, eggs and vanilla. Add dry ingredients, mix well, then stir in nuts and raisins. Add either coconut, apple or applesauce and drop by teaspoonfuls onto lightly oiled cookie sheets. Bake at 375 degrees for 10-12 minutes and cool thoroughly before storing.

Preparation time: 1 1/2 hours      Yield: About 200 cookies
   Hint: These are a soft cookie; dough will not be stiff; cookies freeze well.

Mrs. Weldon Long
Sterling, Illinois

## CARROT-RAISIN CHEWS

1 c. butter or margarine
1/2 c. honey
2 eggs
1 tsp. vanilla
1 c. whole wheat flour
1 tsp. baking powder
1 tsp. cinnamon

1/2 tsp. salt
1/2 tsp. nutmeg
1/4 tsp. cloves
2 1/2 c. oats
2 c. shredded carrots
3/4 c. raisins
1/2 c. chopped nuts

Cream butter and honey. Blend in eggs and vanilla. Add flour, baking powder, cinnamon, salt, nutmeg and cloves. Stir in oats, carrots, raisins and nuts. Drop by teaspoonfuls and bake on greased cookie sheets at 350 degrees for 12-15 minutes. Cool. Store in loosely covered container.

Preparation time: 45 minutes          Yield: 5 dozen

Terry L. Praznik
Prairie Village, Kansas


## BANANA-OATMEAL COOKIES

1 c. honey
3/4 c. butter or margarine
1 egg, well beaten
1 tsp. soda
1/2 tsp. nutmeg
1 tsp. cinnamon

1 c. ripe mashed banana
1 1/2 c. sifted whole wheat flour
1 c. raisins
1 3/4 c. oats
1/2 c. chopped nuts

Cream honey and butter, then mix in all ingredients in order. Drop by teaspoonfuls onto greased cookie sheets. Bake at 350 degrees for 15 minutes. Watch closely and remove when the edges are brown; cool on wire racks.

Preparation time: 45 minutes          Yield: 5-6 dozen

Terry L. Praznik
Prairie Village, Kansas

## COOKIE MONSTERS

1/2 c. butter
1/4 c. oil
1/2 c. honey
2 eggs
2 pureed bananas

2 c. granola
1 1/2 c. whole wheat or unbleached
  flour
1 tsp. baking powder
1 tsp. cinnamon
1 c. unsweetened carob chips
  (optional)

Cream butter and oil. Add honey and cream into butter. Beat in eggs and bananas. Mix in dry ingredients, beating until well mixed. Stir in carob chips if desired. Bake at 350 degrees for 17 minutes or until edges are golden brown.

Preparation time: 10 minutes +
                  baking time

Yield: 3-4 dozen

Kathy Ortmann
Marcus, Iowa


## DATE BARS

16 oz. pkg. dates
1 1/2 c. unsweetened coconut
1/2 c. butter
1/2 c. water

2 1/2 c. old fashioned oats
2/3 c. pecans, chopped
1 tsp. vanilla

Cook the dates, coconut, butter and water over medium high heat until the mixture boils and the dates can easily be mashed with a spoon. This can also be cooked in a microwave oven on high until the dates can be mashed easily. Then add oats, nuts, and vanilla. Mix well. Pour into a 9-inch square pan that has been buttered. Refrigerate several hours and then cut in squares.

Preparation time: 20 minutes +
                  refrigeration

Yield: 16-24 bars

Cathy Burriesci
Knoxville, Tennessee

## HUNGARIAN BARS

1 c. butter or margarine
1/3 c. fructose
1 egg
2 1/4 c. unbleached flour

1 1/2 c. chopped walnuts
3/4 c. fructose
1 1/2 tsp. cinnamon
4 egg whites

Preheat oven to 325 degrees and oil a jelly roll pan. Beat together butter, fructose and egg; add flour and press into pan. Bake for 15 minutes.

Meanwhile, mix walnuts, 3/4 cup fructose, cinnamon and egg whites in a 2-quart saucepan. Heat to boiling, stirring constantly. Spread over hot crust and bake an additional 20 minutes until topping appears dry. Cool slightly, then cut into bars.

Preparation time: 45 minutes          Yield: About 50

Mrs. Norman E. Lemay
North Glenn, Colorado

## HONEY-CAROB BROWNIES

1 1/3 c. honey
1 c. oil
4 eggs
2 tsp. vanilla

1 c. carob powder
1 c. nuts, chopped
2 c. whole wheat flour

Blend all ingredients in order given. Turn dough into buttered 12x9x2-inch pan. Bake 25-30 minutes at 350 degrees. Do not overbake.

Preparation time: 35 minutes          Yield: 16-24 brownies
Hint: When brownies come from the oven, cover immediately with foil to drive the moisture in. Yum!

Carole Jasinek
San Diego, California

## ZUCCHINI BROWNIES

3/4 c. honey
1/4 c. oil
2 eggs
2 c. unbleached white flour
1 tsp. cinnamon

1 tsp. soda
2 Tbsp. carob powder
1/2 tsp. salt
2 1/2 c. grated zucchini
1 c. unsweetened carob chips
1 c. chopped walnuts

Cream honey, oil, and eggs. Sift flour, cinnamon, soda, carob powder and salt; add to honey mixture. Mix well. Stir in zucchini. Put in 10 1/2 x 15 1/2-inch greased pan. Sprinkle with topping of 1 cup carob chips, and 1 cup chopped nuts (walnuts). Bake at 350 degrees for 30 minutes or until done.

Preparation time: 40 minutes          Yield: 24-30 servings
Hint: Good plain or frosted with Cream Cheese Icing.

Mary J. Steffens
Marcus, Iowa


## YOGURT APPLE CRISP

2 Tbsp. whole wheat flour
1/2 c. honey
1 c. yogurt
1 tsp. cinnamon

1/2 tsp. salt
1 tsp. vanilla
4 c. peeled, chopped apples

Combine flour, honey, yogurt, cinnamon, salt and vanilla, making a thin batter. Add batter to apples, then pour into a lightly greased 9-inch pie pan. Bake at 350 degrees for one hour, then add topping.

**Topping:**

2/3 c. oats
1/4 c. honey

1/4 c. melted butter or margarine
1 tsp. cinnamon

Combine ingredients and sprinkle over apples. Increase temperature to 400 degrees and bake an additional 15 minutes.

Preparation time: 1 1/2 hours          Yield: 8-10 servings
Hint: This recipe can be doubled and cooked in a lightly greased 9x9-inch pan, or baked in a pie shell. If baked as a pie, bake 15 minutes at 400 degrees; reduce heat to 350 degrees and bake 45 minutes. Continue with topping instructions as directed.

Cindy Mahan
Spokane, Washington

# HONEY ICE CREAM

3 eggs                              3 c. cream
1/2 c. honey                        2 tsp. vanilla
4 c. milk                           1 c. milk

Beat eggs and honey until very thick (about 1 minute if using a blender). Add 4 cups milk, cream, beat well, then add vanilla and remaining milk. Freeze in a 1-gallon electric freezer as directed.

Preparation time: 15 minutes +        Yield: About 1 gallon
                  freezer time


# BAKED HONEY CUSTARD

3 eggs                              2 1/2 c. milk
1/4 c. honey or maple syrup         Ground nutmeg or cinnamon
1 tsp. vanilla

Beat eggs, honey, and vanilla with a wire whisk. Stir in milk. Pour in glass baking dish or six custard cups. Sprinkle with either spice. Set in pan of hot water. Bake large dish at 325 degrees for 1 hour and cups at 350 degrees for 40-45 minutes.

Preparation time: 1 hour            Yield: 6 servings
                  10 minutes

Linda Andrews
Marcus, Iowa


# CUSTARD

4 eggs, slightly beaten             2 1/2 c. milk
1/2 c. fructose or honey            1 tsp. vanilla
1/2 tsp. salt                       Grated nutmeg

Beat eggs slightly and add fructose and salt, then add milk and vanilla. Strain custard mixture into custard dishes; sprinkle generously with nutmeg. Bake at 375 degrees for 15 minutes, then at 350 degrees for about 30 minutes or until knife inserted comes out clean.

Preparation time: 1 hour            Yield: 6 servings

Margriet Olson
Marcus, Iowa

POTPOURRI

# APPLE CIDER SYRUP

3/4 c. honey
2 Tbsp. cornstarch
1/4 tsp. cinnamon
1/4 tsp. nutmeg

2 c. apple cider
2 Tbsp. lemon juice
1/4 c. butter

In saucepan mix honey, cornstarch and spices. Stir in apple cider and lemon juice. Cook, stirring constantly, until mixture thickens and boils. Boil and stir about 1 minute. Remove from heat and stir in butter. (Works great in the microwave too!)

Preparation time: 10 minutes          Yield: 3 cups
     Hint: Great on pancakes or ice cream. Can be stored in the refrigerator.

Cindy Bailey
Spirit Lake, Iowa


# CHUCK STEAK MARINADE

1 1/2 c. oil
3/4 c. soy sauce or tamari
1/2 c. fresh lemon juice
1/2 c. wine vinegar
1/4 c. Worcestershire sauce

2 Tbsp. dry mustard
1 Tbsp. pepper
2 1/2 tsp. salt
1 1/2 tsp. parsley flakes
2 fresh garlic cloves

Mix well and marinate chuck steak 2-3 hours or overnight in refrigerator. Especially good grilled outside.

Preparation time: 15 minutes          Yield: About 1 quart
     Hint: Marinade may be re-used within 2 weeks.

Claudia Tanner
Eaton Rapids, Michigan


# FRUIT LEATHER

To each cup of fruit, add 4 tablespoons honey and a dash of cinnamon. Puree in blender 1 cup at a time. Put Saran Wrap on cookie sheet and pour 1/4 inch thick. Cook at 150 degrees for 8 hours. Peel off cookie sheet when cool.

Cheryl Patrick
Harrison, Arkansas

## HONEY DRESSING

1 tsp. dry mustard
1 tsp. celery seed
1 tsp. paprika
1/4 tsp. salt
2/3 c. honey

5 Tbsp. vinegar
1 Tbsp. lemon juice
1 tsp. grated onion
1 c. oil

Mix dry ingredients in blender jar. Add honey, vinegar, lemon juice and onion; blend. Add oil very slowly, blending as you add. Store in refrigerator; shake before using.

Preparation time: 10 minutes          Yield: 2 cups
    Hint: This is excellent on fresh fruit.


## MAYONNAISE (SALAD DRESSING)

1 egg
1/2 tsp. salt
1/4 tsp. cayenne pepper
2 Tbsp. honey

4 tsp. apple cider vinegar
7 tsp. lemon juice
1 1/4 c. oil

Put all ingredients into a blender, except the oil. When they are well blended, slowly, very slowly add the oil. Soon the mixture will become thickened. If you want it to be sweet, add a little honey.

Preparation time: 10 minutes          Yield: 1 1/3 cups mayonnaise

Mary J. Steffens
Marcus, Iowa


## SALAD DRESSING

Juice from 2 lemons
4 Tbsp. homemade mayonnaise

4 Tbsp. honey or fructose
Dash salt

Blend in blender.

Preparation time: 5 minutes          Yield: A little over 1 cup

Cheryl Patrick
Harrison, Arkansas

## SLAW DRESSING

1 c. homemade mayonnaise      3 tsp. prepared mustard
1/3 c. honey

Mix all ingredients in blender. Refrigerate, use as needed. (Keeps well for weeks.)

Preparation time: 15 minutes      Yield: Short pint

Virginia McWilliams
Atlanta, Texas


## CARROT AND MUSHROOM RELISH

1 lb. medium mushrooms      1/4 c. water
2 medium carrots, cut into      1 1/2 tsp. fructose
    1/8 inch strips      1 tsp. salt
1 medium onion, sliced      1 Tbsp. minced parsley
1/4 c. red wine vinegar

Early in day or 1 day ahead, cut each mushroom into quarters. In a medium sized saucepan, combine all ingredients except parsley. Bring mixture to boiling over medium heat. Reduce heat and simmer, covered, for 8-10 minutes, until crisp-tender. Stir in parsley. Pour mixture into bowl, cover and chill (4 hours at least), stirring occasionally.

Preparation time: 15 minutes +      Yield: 6 servings
             chilling time

Marsha Hills
Peace River, Alberta, Canada


## HONEY COCONUT BALLS

1/3 c. butter or margarine      2 c. chopped nuts
3/4 c. light honey      1 1/2 c. powdered milk
3/4 c. unsweetened coconut      6 oz. unsweetened carob chips
2 tsp. vanilla      1/4 stick paraffin

Mix butter and honey, warm slightly. Add coconut and vanilla, then nuts and powdered milk, mixing well after each addition. Shape into balls and place on waxed paper. Melt carob chips and paraffin in double boiler or microwave; dip candies in, then set on waxed paper to harden.

Preparation time: 20 minutes      Yield: 3-4 dozen
    Hint: To avoid using paraffin, substitute two 3-ounce unsweetened carob candy bars, melted, for the chips and paraffin.

Pat Jackson
Russellville, Arkansas

## SUPER FUDGE

1 c. honey
1 c. natural style peanut
  butter
1 c. carob powder

1 c. unhulled sesame seeds
1 c. sunflower seeds
1/2 c. unsweetened coconut
1/2 c. date pieces

Warm honey and peanut butter to a creamy consistency; quickly add other ingredients. Pour into a buttered 8x8-inch pan, refrigerate, and cut into squares.

Preparation time: 20 minutes     Yield: 16 pieces
   Hint: If this cools before you get it mixed well enough, warm it up again.

Mrs. R.D. Dieter
Waterville, Ohio


## CAROB CANDY

1 1/2 c. rolled oats, granola
  or chopped nuts (or half
  cup of each of these)
1 c. natural style peanut
  butter

3/4 c. raisins
1/3 c. honey
1/4 c. carob powder
1/2 tsp. vanilla

In a large bowl, combine all ingredients and mix until smooth. Form into balls with your hands, (about the size of a walnut).

Preparation time: 20 minutes     Yield: 24 balls
   Hint: It is easier to mix the ingredients if the peanut butter, honey, carob powder and vanilla were mixed together first.

Judy McCool
Covington, Tennessee

## BREAKFAST PEANUT BUTTER BALLS

2 c. natural style peanut
  butter
1/2 c. honey

1 1/2 c. toasted wheat germ
1 1/2 c. powdered milk
1/2 tsp. salt (more if desired)

Mix ingredients well with a fork or pastry blender. Form into 1-inch balls (a meat ball former is handy for this).

Preparation time: 20 minutes      Yield: 38-40 balls
    Hint: If the peanut butter is dry because it wasn't stirred well, add 1-2 tablespoons oil. These freeze well, in fact they're delicious frozen. Try using this mixture as a crust for an ice cream pie!

Susan M. Walker
Jackson, Michigan


## PEANUT BUTTER BARS

1 c. honey (or less to taste)
  warmed
1 c. natural peanut butter
2 c. nonfat dry milk

1 c. coconut, unsweetened
2 c. unhulled sesame seeds or
  sunflower seeds

Mix all ingredients together. Fun for children to do with their hands. Press into 9x13-inch buttered pan or roll into balls.

Preparation time: 15 minutes      Yield: 35 cookies

Beth Miller
Emporia, Kansas


## ROMAN SOLDIERS SNACK

1/4 c. butter
1/2 c. unhulled sesame seeds
1 c. unsweetened coconut

1/2 Tbsp. vanilla
1/4 c. honey

In large frying pan over low heat, melt butter. Stir in sesame seeds and coconut. Stir over low heat 15 minutes. Remove from stove and mix in vanilla and honey. Refrigerate until stiff enough for balls. Roll into balls. (Refrigerate what you don't eat.)

Preparation time: 30 minutes +      Yield: 36 balls
                 refrigeration
    Hint: These can also be spread in a buttered square pan, chilled, and cut into rectangular bars.

Mrs. R.D. Dieter
Waterville, Ohio

## RITA'S GRANOLA

4 c. oats
1 1/3 c. wheat germ
1/3 c. bran
1/4 c. powdered milk
1 1/2 Tbsp. cinnamon
1/3 c. oil

1/2 c. honey
1 Tbsp. vanilla
1/2 c. sunflower seeds or raw nuts
1/2 c. raisins or other dried fruit
1/2 c. unhulled sesame seeds

In large bowl mix first 5 ingredients. In a saucepan, combine oil, honey and vanilla. Add these to the dry ingredients and stir until coated, (hand mix). Spread mixture on long baking sheet. Bake at 250 degrees for 1 hour or 300 degrees for 30 minutes. Turn with spatula from time to time. When finished, add raisins, seeds, etc. Store in airtight container.

Preparation time: Up to 1
hour 15 minutes

Yield: 2 quarts

Rita Hartel
Murray, Nebraska

## GRANOLA

4 c. oats
1 c. mixed chopped nuts
1/2 c. each sunflower seeds,
unhulled sesame seeds,
wheat germ

1/4 c. powdered milk
1/2 c. oil
1/2 c. honey
1 tsp. cinnamon

Combine the first three ingredients. Mix oil, honey and cinnamon in saucepan and heat. Add to the cereal mixture. Bake at 300 degrees for 30 minutes. Stir occasionally. If you double the recipe, bake for 45 minutes.

Preparation time: 35-50 minutes     Yield: 3 quarts

Rosemary Wibe
Marcus, Iowa

## EASY GRANOLA

7 c. oats
1 c. rolled wheat
1 c. wheat germ
1 c. peanuts
1 c. unhulled sesame seeds

1 c. sunflower seeds
1/2 c. powdered milk
1 c. shredded unsweetened
  coconut
1/2 c. oil
3/4 c. honey

In a large baking pan or Dutch oven, toast the oats and wheat in a 400 degree oven, stirring every few minutes. Add wheat germ, seeds, nuts, milk, and coconut. Toast complete mixture 5 minutes. Stir in remaining ingredients and toast another 5 minutes. Store in loosely covered jar.

Preparation time: 30-40 minutes     Yield: 3 - 3 1/2 quarts

Janet Hillstrand
Harlan, Iowa


## FAVORITE GRANOLA

6 c. oats
1 c. soy flour
1 c. unhulled sesame seeds
1 c. wheat germ
1 c. nonfat dry milk (optional)
1 c. chopped nuts

1 c. unsweetened coconut
1/2 c. brewer's yeast
1 c. oil
1 c. honey
1 Tbsp. vanilla

Mix dry ingredients in a large (turkey) roasting pan. Blend and add oil, honey and vanilla, drizzling and stirring until ingredients are moistened. Bake at 300 degrees, stirring at 10 minute intervals once edges have begun to brown, until toasted throughout.

Preparation time: 1 hour     Yield: 3-4 quarts
    Hint: Top with fresh bananas and strawberries.

Suzanne Ratliff
Russellville, Arkansas

## SPICED GRANOLA

4 c. oats
4 oz. shredded unsweetened
  coconut
1/2 c. unhulled sesame seeds
1/2 c. raw sunflower seeds

1/2 c. wheat germ
1 1/2 tsp. cinnamon
1 tsp. nutmeg
1/2 c. honey
1/2 c. oil
1 c. raisins

Combine the first 7 ingredients. Add honey and oil; mix well. Pour into two baking pans and bake in preheated 350 degree oven until golden...... about 18 minutes. Stir occasionally.

Cool and crumble. Stir in raisins. Store in tightly-covered container. Keeps best in refrigerator. Makes about 10 cups. Eat plain or serve with milk for a delicious and nutritious treat.

Preparation time: 40 minutes          Yield: 1 1/2 quarts

Gay Strub
Marcus, Iowa

## SUNSHINE MUESLI (SWISS OATMEAL)

3 oranges, peeled,
  chopped coarsely
2 c. old fashioned
  oats, uncooked
1/2 c. raisins

1/3 c. chopped nuts
2 Tbsp. honey
1/4 c. milk, for drier
  crunchier cereal or 1 c. milk,
  for soft cereal

Combine all the ingredients. Cover and refrigerate at least 8 hours. (Usually made the night before so ready for breakfast). Mix well and serve.

Preparation time: 15 minutes +          Yield: 8-10 servings
              overnight

Rita Hartel
Murray, Nebraska

## CROCK POT CINNAMON OATMEAL

3 1/2 c. water
1 1/2 c. oats
1/2 tsp. salt

1 1/2 tsp. cinnamon
1/3 c. raisins

Place all ingredients in a crock pot and turn on low. Leave overnight or approximately 8 hours.

Preparation time: 5 minutes +          Yield: 4 generous servings
              overnight

Mary J. Steffens
Marcus, Iowa

# MINT COOLER

2 medium oranges
1 small lemon
1 tsp. dried mint leaves

2 Tbsp. honey
6 ice cubes
1 c. cold water

To prepare oranges and lemons quickly, wash and peel and then cut across the equator. All pits will be visible for picking out. Put into the blender and process at high speed until liquefied. Add the mint leaves and honey. Process at low speed. Add ice cubes and blend at high speed until well chopped. Add the water and blend at low speed until smooth.

Preparation time: 10 minutes          Yield: 3 cups

Ruth Ann Peters
Harrison, Arkansas

# WEDDING FRUIT PUNCH

2 bananas, pureed in blender
   (or 1 small bottle banana
   juice) with 2 squirts lemon
   juice
12 oz. frozen orange juice
   concentrate, unsweetened

46 oz. can unsweetened pineapple
   juice
2 qt. Diet 7-Up or Shasta Sugar
   Free ginger ale (or apple cider or
   carbonated water)

Puree bananas and lemon juice. Add orange juice concentrate and puree. Add some of pineapple juice and blend (can freeze some of this for ice ring). Add rest of liquid and mix in a large pitcher or punch bowl. Serve chilled.

Preparation time: 10 minutes +          Yield: Approximately 1 gallon
                  chilling or freezer
                  time

Beth Miller
Emporia, Kansas

# YOGURT BANANA BLEND

1 c. plain yogurt
1/4 c. milk
1 small or 1/2 large banana
2 Tbsp. honey, if desired

1 Tbsp. wheat germ
1/8 tsp. almond or vanilla extract
1/2 c. crushed ice or ice cubes
Banana slices for garnish

Blend all ingredients except garnish in blender or malted milk mixer 15-20 seconds. Pour into 14 or 16 ounce serving glass. Garnish with banana slices if desired.

Preparation time: 5 minutes          Yield: 1 serving

Penny Tutton
Leesburg, Florida

# BLENDER WHIRL

1 c. frozen fruit                     3/4 c. buttermilk (or yogurt)
1 tsp. vanilla                        Ice cubes
Sweetener (honey or fructose to taste)

   Put all ingredients into a blender and blend until desired consistency.
The mixture should be thick.
   Always use frozen fruit. To freeze the fruit, cut in chunks, and spread on
cookie sheet, put in freezer until frozen and then pack into bags. The pieces
are individually frozen and easy to use because they don't get "smushy".
   The blender drink can use any fruit that you have frozen: bananas, cut
up chunks of cantaloupe, strawberries, blueberries, whatever.

Preparation time: 5 minutes          Yield: 1 serving

Gay Strub
Marcus, Iowa


# PINEAPPLE PUNCH

1/4 c. pineapple juice                1 tsp. lemon juice
1/4 c. orange juice                   1/4 c. sparkling mineral water
1/4 c. grapefruit juice

   Combine juices and add sparkling mineral water. Serve over ice.

Preparation time: 5 minutes          Yield: 1 serving
   Hint: May be multiplied for large groups.

Mary Lou McCray
Jonesboro, Arkansas


# NUTTY 'NANA SHAKE

1/2 c. milk                           2 Tbsp. natural style peanut butter
1/2 c. crushed ice or cubes           1 Tbsp. honey, if desired
1 small banana or                     1/8 tsp. vanilla extract
   1/2 large banana

   Blend all ingredients in blender or malted milk mixer until ice melts,
about 1 minute. Pour into a 12 or 14 ounce serving glass. Makes one serving.

Preparation time: 5 minutes          Yield: 1 serving

Penny Tutton
Leesburg, Florida

## WASSAIL

| | |
|---|---|
| 2 qt. apple cider | 1 stick whole cinnamon |
| 2 c. unsweetened orange juice | 1 tsp. whole cloves |
| 1 c. lemon juice | Honey to taste |
| 1 (6 oz.) can pineapple juice | |

Combine ingredients and bring to a simmer, covered. Strain and serve hot.

Preparation time: 10 minutes

Yield: 3 1/2 quarts

Karen Shrum
Harrison, Arkansas


## TUESDAY'S BREAKFAST ON THE GO

| | |
|---|---|
| 2 c. unsweetened orange juice | 1/2 c. sliced bananas |
| 1 c. plain yogurt | 1 c. chopped ice |
| 1/2 c. strawberries, washed and capped | Cinnamon |

Place orange juice, yogurt, strawberries and bananas in a blender and blend until smooth. Add chopped ice, blending until smooth. Pour into glasses and top each serving with a pinch of cinnamon.

Preparation time: 10 minutes

Yield: 4 cups

Stacie Pearce
Jacksonville, Florida


## ZUCCHINI ROUNDS

| | |
|---|---|
| 1/3 c. biscuit mix (from *Feasting Naturally*) | 2 slightly beaten eggs |
| 1/4 c. grated Parmesan cheese | 2 c. shredded unpared zucchini (2 medium zucchini) |
| 1/8 tsp. pepper | 2 Tbsp. butter |

In mixing bowl, stir together biscuit mix, cheese and pepper. Stir in beaten eggs just until moistened, then fold in zucchini. In 10-inch skillet, melt butter over medium heat. Using 2 tablespoons mixture for each round, cook four rounds at a time about 2-3 minutes on each side, or until brown. Keep warm while cooking remaining rounds.

Preparation time: 30 minutes

Yield: 12 rounds (6 servings)

Judy Beemer
Sharon Springs, Kansas

## ZUCCHINI APPETIZERS

3 c. thinly sliced unpeeled
  zucchini (about 4 small)
1 c. "Bisquick"-type baking
  mix
1/2 c. onion, finely chopped
1/2 c. Parmesan cheese
1/2 c. oil
4 eggs, slightly beaten

2 Tbsp. snipped parsley
1/2 tsp. salt
1/2 tsp. seasoned salt
1/2 tsp. dried marjoram or
  oregano
1 clove garlic, chopped fine
Dash of pepper

Preheat oven to 350 degrees; oil a 9x13-inch pan. Mix all ingredients together and pour into pan. Bake about 25 minutes, until golden. Slice into 1 1/2-inch pieces and serve.

Preparation time: 40 minutes        Yield: 8-10 servings
  Hint: To make your own Bisquick mix, combine these ingredients and mix thoroughly in a food processor.

9 c. flour (unbleached
  and whole wheat)
1/3 c. baking powder
1 Tbsp. salt

2 1/2 tsp. cream of tartar
1 tsp. soda
1 1/2 c. powdered milk
2 1/4 c. vegetable shortening

Mrs. Norman E. Lemay
North Glenn, Colorado


## TINY PIZZAS

1 can tomato paste
1 1/2 tsp. Worcestershire sauce
1/2 tsp. salt
1/2 tsp. garlic salt

Biscuit dough for 5-6 biscuits
1 lb. ground beef
1/2 c. grated cheese
Oregano

Combine first 4 ingredients; mix well. Roll or stretch each biscuit to a thin circle about 4 inches in diameter. Cover each with a layer of uncooked ground beef, spread with tomato paste mixture, sprinkle with cheese and oregano. Place on an ungreased baking sheet and bake at 425 degrees for 10 minutes.

Preparation time: 30 minutes        Yield: 5-6 servings
  Hint: Use frozen biscuit recipe on page 17 to save time.

Mrs. Kathy Horton
Ocean Springs, Mississippi

# SUMMER SAUSAGE

5 lb. ground beef (expensive
cut not necessary)
5 rounded tsp. Morton's tender
quick salt
3 tsp. garlic salt
4 tsp. mustard seed

5 tsp. coarse ground black pepper
6 tsp. hickory smoke salt
1 Tbsp. Accent (optional)
1 tsp. liquid smoke
1/2 tsp. cayenne pepper

Mix and refrigerate; keep covered. Mix once a day for 3 days. On 4th day, form into 10 rolls (2 1/2 inches in diameter). Place on rack in broiler pan and cook in oven 8 hours at 175-200 degrees; turn once after 4 hours. (Be sure to cook on rack so grease will drain off.)

Preparation time: 4 days          Yield: 10 rolls
Hint: This is excellent especially around holidays to have on hand to serve on crackers with mustard, and to give away to friends. This can be frozen if hamburger has not been frozen. Keeps in refrigerator for 4-6 weeks if covered.

Jan Berryhill
Richmond, Virginia


# PARTY CHEESE BALL

2 (8 oz.) pkg. cream cheese
2 c. shredded sharp Cheddar
cheese
1 Tbsp. chopped pimento
1 Tbsp. chopped green pepper
1 Tbsp. or more chopped onion
(to taste)

2 tsp. Worcestershire sauce
(optional)
1 tsp. lemon juice
Dash cayenne
Dash salt
Finely chopped nuts

Combine softened cream cheese and Cheddar cheese, mixing until well blended. Add remaining ingredients except nuts. Mix well. Chill. Shape into ball. Roll in nuts. Serve with whole wheat crackers.

Preparation time: 15 minutes          Yield: 1 large cheese ball

Kathleen Hackman
London, Arkansas

## WHEAT GERM CHEESE SPREAD

2 c. grated sharp cheese
1/2 c. chopped apple
1/2 c. chopped walnuts
1/2 c. chopped celery
1/2 c. shredded carrots
1/3 c. homemade mayonnaise

2 Tbsp. chopped raisins
2 Tbsp. chopped dates
1 Tbsp. wheat germ
1 tsp. lemon juice
1 tsp. Worcestershire sauce
(optional)

Combine all ingredients, mixing well. Chill overnight. Serve with crisp raw vegetables.

Preparation time: 15 minutes        Yield: 1 1/4 cups
Hint: Is great with wholegrain crackers, too.

Genevieve Russell
Dallas, Texas

## CONFETTI DIP

8 oz. cream cheese, softened
1/2 c. sour cream
1/2 c. bunch chopped green
  onions
1 medium tomato, finely chopped

1 small green pepper, chopped fine
1 tsp. dry mustard
1 tsp. salt
1/2 tsp. pepper

Mix together and serve with fresh vegetable strips such as green pepper strips, carrot and celery strips, squash and cucumber slices and cauliflowerets.

Preparation time: 10 minutes        Yield: 2 c. dip
Hint: For an especially pretty centerpiece, hollow out a purple cabbage and serve the dip inside, surrounded by vegetables.

Carol Ashberry
Cabot, Arkansas

## GUACAMOLE DIP

2 ripe avocados, mashed
1 medium tomato, peeled
  and diced
3 Tbsp. minced onion
1 clove garlic, minced

2 Tbsp. oil
1/2 tsp. salt
1/4 tsp. black pepper
1 tsp. lemon juice
3 dashes hot pepper sauce

Blend all ingredients together thoroughly.

Preparation time: 10 minutes        Yield: 1 1/2 cups
Serving Tip: Arrange sliced tomatoes and corn tortilla chips on bed of lettuce. Top with guacamole or put in center of arrangement.

Karen Reynolds
Siloam Springs, Arkansas

## PIZZA DIP

1 tsp. onion salt
1 tsp. garlic salt
1 tsp. milk
2 pkg. (8 oz. each) cream
  cheese, softened
8 oz. tomato sauce
1/2 tsp. basil

1/2 tsp. oregano
1 small onion, chopped fine
1 small green pepper, chopped fine
3 1/4 oz. chopped black olives
4 oz. Mozzarella cheese,
  shredded fine

The night before serving, combine onion salt, garlic salt, and milk to make a paste. Blend the paste with the softened cream cheese and spread the mixture on a Pyrex pizza pan or decorative dish. Mix tomato sauce with basil and oregano and spread over cream cheese. Combine onion, green pepper and olives and sprinkle over the tomato sauce; sprinkle cheese on last. Refrigerate until serving time, preferably overnight. Serve with party crackers or vegetables.

Preparation time: 10 minutes +
                   refrigeration time
Yield: 1 pizza

Hint: To store in the refrigerator, place toothpicks upright in dip, cover with plastic wrap.

Carol Ashberry
Cabot, Arkansas


## FRESH FRUIT DIP

2 c. Ricotta cheese
Dash cinnamon

6 Tbsp. unsweetened orange juice
  (or more if desired for thinner
  consistency)

Mix in blender until smooth and refrigerate until ready to use. Serve with pineapple chunks, apple slices, cantaloupe chunks, strawberries, banana slices, and grapes.

Preparation time: 5 minutes
Yield: 2 1/4 cups

Cathy Burriesci
Knoxville, Tennessee

## JIM'S HOT SAUCE
### "Like Ro-tel!"

1 qt. canned tomatoes
1 (16 oz.) can tomato sauce
1/2 c. white vinegar
1 (4 oz.) can green chilies
2-3 canned jalapeno peppers
1 medium onion, chopped

1/8 c. oil
1/4 tsp. oregano
1/8 tsp. savory
1/8 tsp. garlic powder
Salt to taste

Mix ingredients in a big bowl then put through a blender or food processor to mix well. It may also be mashed by hand.

Preparation time: 10 minutes        Yield: 2 quarts
Hint: Two quarts of hot sauce is a lot—unless you are a real hot sauce fan, you may want to halve or quarter this recipe. This is like a picante sauce.

Jim Ashberry
Cabot, Arkansas


## "RO-TEL"
### (TOMATO HOT SAUCE)

4 oz. can green chilies
  (Old El Paso)
2-3 jalapeno peppers, canned
1 fresh medium onion, chopped
16 oz. tomato sauce

1/2 c. wine vinegar
1/4 tsp. oregano
1/8 tsp. garlic powder
1/8 tsp. savory
1/8 c. oil
Salt to taste

Mix ingredients in a big bowl. Put through a blender briefly to mix. Freezes well. A good base for chili sauce or cheese dips.

Preparation time: 15 minutes        Yield: About 3 cups
Hint: This is more concentrated than "Jim's Hot Sauce".

Carol Ashberry
Cabot, Arkansas

# FRUIT FREEZE

1 can unsweetened pineapple
  with juice
2 bananas

1 c. apple juice or orange juice
1/4 c. honey
2 egg whites

    Place pineapple in blender until smooth. Add chunks of bananas, juice and honey. Blend and pour into pan and place in freezer until half frozen. Beat two egg whites until stiff and fold into the half frozen fruit mixture. Spoon into plastic cups and place in freezer. It is best to let them unthaw a little in refrigerator before serving. Other fruits may be substituted. Good summer toddler treats.

Preparation time: 10 minutes +
              freezing

Yield: 6-8 servings

Jeralyn Volkert
Marcus, Iowa


# APPLE BUTTER

16 c. unsweetened applesauce
4 c. honey

1 c. cider
2 Tbsp. cinnamon

    Mix together. Put into a large roasting pan or something large and flat. Bake at 200 degrees for 4 or 5 hours or until a little butter that has cooled on a plate is of good consistency. Stir occasionally. This recipe may be cut in half. May be stored in refrigerator for some time or canned.

Preparation time: 5 1/2 hours     Yield: 3 - 3 1/2 quarts
    Hint: The honey that is used should be very, very light and mild.

Janet Shumaker
Delta, Ohio


# RASPBERRY PRESERVES

1 pt. raspberries, washed      1 c. honey (best if very mild)

    Cook on top of very slow stove until desired consistency is reached. A small portion may be cooled on a plate for quicker use.

Preparation time: 45 minutes -    Yield: 1 c. preserves
            1 hour
    Hint: This recipe is very good made with strawberries, too.

Janet Shumaker
Delta, Ohio

## STRAWBERRY FREEZER JAM

**6 qt. strawberries**                    **3 c. honey**
**6 pkg. Knox gelatin**

Crush strawberries—if possible, allow them to set for 4 hours. Remove 1 cup of juice. Heat 1 cup juice, Knox gelatin and 3 cups of honey just to boiling. Pour hot mixture over crushed strawberries and mix well (at least 2 minutes). Pour in jam jars and freeze. May refrigerate for a while only. May add a dash of lemon if desired.

Preparation time: 5 hours          Yield: 6-7 pints

Rosemary Wibe
Marcus, Iowa

KID'S CORNER

## FRESH APPLE SLUSH

**1 (6 oz.) can apple juice
  concentrate, frozen**

**1 c. cold water
1/2 c. peeled, diced apple**

1. Prepare the apple.
2. Put everything into a blender.
3. Cover and blend on high for 10-15 seconds.
4. With blender running, add 6-8 ice cubes one at a time....blend until thick.

Preparation time: 5 minutes          Yield: 3-4 servings

Deane Inness
Tucson, Arizona


## TOASTED PUMPKIN SEEDS

**1 Tbsp. melted butter or
  margarine**

**2 c. pumpkin seeds**

1. Turn the oven on to 250 degrees.
2. Place pumpkin seeds in a flat pan.
3. Roast for about 30 minutes or until lightly browned, stirring several times.
4. Remove from oven and cool.

Preparation time: 30 minutes          Yield: 2 cups seeds

Kathy Ortmann
Marcus, Iowa


## MAPLE GLAZED NUTS

**1/2 c. 100% maple syrup or
  honey
1 tsp. cinnamon
1 Tbsp. butter**

**1/4 tsp. salt
1 1/2 tsp. vanilla
2 c. walnuts**

1. In a heavy skillet, stir together syrup, cinnamon, butter and salt.
2. Cook and stir over medium heat until it becomes brown and starts to thicken.
3. Add vanilla and nuts, and toss until evenly glazed.
4. Spoon onto waxed paper and cool.

   Preparation time: 15 minutes          Yield: 2 cups

Linda Andrews
Marcus, Iowa

## CRACK-O-SUN JACK

1/2 c. unpopped corn
1/2 c. sunflower seeds

1/2 c. roasted peanuts
3 Tbsp. oil
1 c. honey

1. Pop corn, then set aside in a large mixing bowl. Remove any unpopped corn before going on to Step 2.
2. Lightly saute sunflower seeds and peanuts in oil until lightly browned.
3. Stir honey into frying pan with nuts and seeds, and simmer over low heat for several minutes.
4. Pour honey, seeds, and nuts over popcorn and toss gently until thoroughly coated.

Preparation time: 15 minutes        Yield: 3 quarts

Mary Lou McCray
Jonesboro, Arkansas


## POPCORN SNACK MIX

1/2 c. melted butter
1/2 c. honey
1 Tbsp. grated orange peel
(more if desired)

1/4 tsp. nutmeg
5 quarts popped popcorn
1 c. sunflower seeds

1. Turn the oven on to 375 degrees.
2. Pop the popcorn.
3. Place the popcorn in 2 large rectangular pans, being careful not to put any unpopped corn in with the popped corn.
4. Melt the butter in a saucepan over medium heat.
5. Add the honey, orange peel and nutmeg to the butter.
6. Add the sunflower seeds to the popcorn.
7. Pour the butter mixture over the popcorn and sunflower seeds, tossing and stirring with a fork so popcorn is coated with butter.
8. Bake at 375 degrees for 30 minutes.
9. Remove from oven and cool.

Preparation time: 30 minutes        Yield: 2 large rectangle pans of mix

Cathy Bodell
Fullerton, California

## CAROB YUMMIES

2 Tbsp. carob powder
1/3 c. honey
2 Tbsp. milk
1/3 c. natural style peanut butter

2 c. granola
1/2 c. unsweetened coconut
1/2 c. chopped peanuts (optional)

1. Combine carob, honey and milk in saucepan.
2. Bring carob mixture to a boil and boil about a minute.
3. Remove from heat.
4. Stir in peanut butter, granola, coconut and peanuts.
5. Drop by teaspoonfuls onto waxed paper to cool.
6. Refrigerate any leftovers.

Preparation time: 30 minutes          Yield: 3 dozen

Marilyn B. Hurt
Manassas, Virginia


## RAISIN SESAME SEED CANDY

2 1/2 c. (15 oz. box) raisins
1 c. unhulled sesame seeds

4 Tbsp. carob powder
Unsweetened coconut

1. Grind raisins and sesame seeds together in a food grinder.
2. Mix in carob powder thoroughly.
3. Form small balls (buttering hands if necessary to keep from sticking).
4. Roll in coconut.

Preparation time: 15 minutes          Yield: 2 1/2 - 3 dozen
    Hint: This recipe works nicely in a food processor.

Cathy Burriesci
Knoxville, Tennessee

## JENNY'S FAMOUS MUFFINS

| | |
|---|---|
| 2 1/4 c. whole wheat flour | 1/2 c. honey |
| 1 tsp. salt | 1 c. buttermilk |
| 1 tsp. soda | 1 egg |
| 1 tsp. baking powder | 1 (3 oz.) pkg. unsweetened carob |
| 1/2 c. oil | chips |

1. Turn the oven on to 400 degrees.
2. Measure the flour, salt, soda and baking powder into a bowl.
3. Crack the egg into a small bowl and remove any shells.
4. Combine the oil, honey, buttermilk and egg in a pitcher and stir until blended.
5. Add the liquid ingredients to the flour mixture and stir until well blended.
6. Add the carob chips to the batter and stir.
7. Line 12 muffin cups with muffin papers and pour enough batter to fill each one about 2/3 full.
8. Bake at 400 degrees for 15 minutes. Remove and serve hot.

Preparation time: 20 minutes      Yield: 12 muffins
    Hint: These are famous because they never stick to the paper.

Jennifer Pickard
Harrison, Arkansas


## BIG BIRD BANANA BREAD

| | |
|---|---|
| 1/4 c. butter | 3/4 c. honey |
| 3 peeled ripe bananas | 1/2 tsp. soda |
| 1 1/2 c. whole wheat flour | |

1. Preheat oven to 350 degrees.
2. Melt the butter over low heat in a pan.
3. Place bananas in a bowl and mash with a fork.
4. Add butter to bananas.
5. Add remaining ingredients to bananas and butter.
6. Stir everything well until it is mixed thoroughly.
7. Pour mix into an oiled loaf pan and bake for 50-60 minutes. Test with a toothpick after 50 minutes—if the toothpick comes out clean the bread is done.
8. Cool before cutting.

Preparation time: 1 hour          Yield: 1 loaf
            15 minutes
    Hint: You may want to reduce the amount of honey a bit.

## QUICK BLENDER WAFFLES

| | |
|---|---|
| 1 Tbsp. oil | 1/2 c. whole wheat flour |
| 1 egg | 1/2 c. unbleached flour |
| 2 Tbsp. honey | 2 tsp. baking powder |
| 1/2 - 3/4 c. milk | 2 Tbsp. oil |

1. Season the waffle iron with 1 tablespoon oil and turn on to heat.
2. Break the egg into a bowl, then check to see if any shell needs to be removed.
3. Place the egg in the blender, put the cover on, and whip until it is light and fluffy.
4. Add the honey, cover, and whip again.
5. Add the milk, flours and baking powder, cover, and mix again.
6. Add the oil, cover, and blend well.
7. Pour just enough batter to make one batch into the waffle iron.
8. Remove when golden brown and serve hot.

Preparation time: 15 minutes          Yield: 3-4 (6-inch) round waffles

Lona L. Yender
Nemaha, Iowa


## "KNOX BLOCKS"

| | |
|---|---|
| 4 c. unsweetened juice | 7 envelopes unflavored gelatin |

1. Dissolve gelatin into 2 cups warmed juice.
2. Cool.
3. Add remaining juice.
4. Pour into a 9x13-inch pan and chill until set.

Preparation time: 10 minutes +          Yield: A 9x13-inch pan of blocks,
                 chilling time                      cut as desired
    Hint: Do not use fresh or frozen pineapple juice as it contains an
enzyme that will prevent gelling.

Carole Shearer
Harrison, Arkansas

## PARMESAN TOAST

**Whole wheat bread**                    **Parmesan cheese**
**Butter**

1. Turn the oven on "broil".
2. Place slices of bread in toaster.
3. Spread bread with butter when toasted.
4. Sprinkle a generous amount of Parmesan cheese on buttered toast.
5. Broil until cheese is bubbly.

Preparation time: 10 minutes          Yield: Any number of servings
                                              as desired
    Hint: This is a super breakfast when everyone has overslept—also great with spaghetti.

Carolyn Hoelscher
Ballwin, Missouri


## STRAWBERRY DELIGHT

**1/2 c. alfalfa sprouts**              **1/2 c. creamy cottage cheese**
**1 whole ripe banana**                 **1 large ripe strawberry**

1. Place sprouts in a pretty bowl.
2. Slice banana and arrange on top.
3. Spoon cottage cheese in the middle.
4. Decorate with a large shiny strawberry.

Preparation time: 5 minutes           Yield: 1 serving
    Hint: Especially delicious for breakfast.

Jennifer Pickard
Harrison, Arkansas


## BREAKFAST IN BED

**1 apple, chunked**                    **1 c. sprouts**
**1 1/2 oz. cream cheese**

1. Put sprouts in two dishes.
2. Chop cream cheese.
3. Put apples on top.

Preparation time: 10 minutes          Yield: 2 servings

Monica Sutton
Harrison, Arkansas

## STRAWBERRY YOGURT

**1 c. plain yogurt**                      **1/2 c. fresh or frozen strawberries**
**3 Tbsp. honey**

1. Place yogurt in blender or food processor.
2. Add honey to yogurt.
3. Blend well.
4. Blend in strawberries.
5. Pour into cups and serve.

Preparation time: 5 minutes          Yield: 2 servings
    Hint: 3-4 tablespoons orange juice concentrate can be substituted for
the berries. This recipe can be tripled and frozen in a 1-quart ice cream
freezer.

Sue Marie Brown
Nashville, Tennessee


## MY FAVORITE SANDWICH

**2 slices whole wheat bread**          **1 tsp. bacon chips**
**2 Tbsp. cream cheese, softened**

1. Spread cream cheese on bread.
2. Sprinkle on bacon chips and put together as a sandwich.

Preparation time: 3 minutes          Yield: 1 serving
    Hint: You may also add 3 tablespoons alfalfa sprouts to each sandwich.

Monica Sutton
Harrison, Arkansas


## YOGURT AND ORANGE JUICE POPSICLES

**1 (12 oz.) can frozen**              **3-4 c. plain yogurt (homemade)**
  **concentrated orange juice**

1. Mix orange juice and yogurt together thoroughly with a fork or wire
   whisk.
2. Freeze in popsicle molds or small cups.
3. I like to add a surprise inside—a peanut, raisin, date, etc.

Preparation time: 5 minutes +          Yield 8-12 popsicles
            freezing time
    Hint: You may want to add a little fructose or honey.

Judy Britton
Richmond, Virginia

## YUMMY POPSICLES

1 (6 oz.) can frozen orange
  juice
1 can water

1/2 c. powdered milk
1 banana, peeled and chunked
1 apple, cored and chunked

1. Prepare fruits and measure ingredients.
2. Place all ingredients in blender.
3. Cover and blend until thoroughly mixed.
4. Add ice cubes until blender is full.

Preparation time: 10 minutes     Yield: Eight 4-oz. servings
    Hint: Makes a slush that can be eaten with a spoon or poured into popsicle containers and frozen.

Matthew Sutton
Harrison, Arkansas

## GREEN PEA CASSEROLE

1 (10 oz.) pkg. frozen peas
3 boiled eggs
1 can cream of mushroom soup

1 jar sliced pimentoes
1/2 c. milk
Wholegrain bread crumbs

1. Turn oven on to 350 degrees.
2. Boil eggs for about 10 minutes in boiling water.
3. Steam peas, covered, until tender in about 2 inches of water.
4. Layer half of the following: peas, sliced boiled eggs, pimentoes, and soup.
5. Repeat step 4.
6. Pour milk over all.
7. Sprinkle bread crumbs on top.
8. Bake, covered, about 20 minutes at 350 degrees, until bubbly.

Preparation time: 30 minutes     Yield: 6 servings

Betty Ann Reynolds
Westville, Oklahoma

# BROWNED CHICKEN AND RICE

1/4 c. butter or margarine
1 can onion soup or
  cream of onion soup
1 soup can of water

1 c. uncooked brown rice
1 tsp. salt
1/4 tsp. pepper
1 cut-up frying chicken

1. Preheat oven to 350 degrees.
2. Put butter in a 9x13-inch glass baking dish and melt it in the oven.
3. In a medium sized bowl, mix soup, water, rice, salt and pepper.
4. Add this mixture to butter and stir to mix evenly.
5. Put chicken pieces on top.
6. Bake, uncovered, for 1 hour. (Chicken will then be brown.)
7. Cover with foil and bake for another 30 minutes, or until rice is tender.

Preparation time: 1 hour
                45 minutes

Yield: 4-6 servings

Betty Ritter
St. Marys, Missouri

**INDEX**

151

153

154

155

## MAIN DISHES, CHEESE

## MAIN DISHES, CHICKEN

## MAIN DISHES, EGGS

157

159

## TOPPINGS

## VEGETABLES

# SPECIAL OFFER

**Great News!** You can now subscribe to the exciting and educational *Feasting Naturally* Newsletter, to be published Jan.-Feb., 1983. This is my way of staying current and in closer touch with you, and I'm very enthusiastic about its release. Each newsletter, published every other month, will feature the following sections:

1. Editorial
2. Cooking Tips
3. Book Review
4. Kid's Corner
5. Nutritional News Briefs
6. Featured Food/Recipes
7. Budget Ideas/Recipes
8. Question and Answer
9. Party/Holiday Ideas or Coupons/Rebates

All the information found in the newsletter will follow the well-established *Feasting Naturally* concept of delicious food that is easy to prepare and completely free of refined sugars, flours and food grains. Send in now for subscription, information and for your free copy of the most current edition (see coupon page).

Please send me the following items from the *Feasting....Naturally* collection:

_____ Copies of *Feasting....Naturally* at $7.95 . . . . . . . . . . _____

_____ Copies of *Feasting Naturally....*
*From Your Own Recipes* at $7.95 . . . . . . . . . . . . . . . _____

_____ Copies of *Feasting Naturally....*
*With Our Friends* at $7.95 . . . . . . . . . . . . . . . . . . . . . _____

_____ Please send me a free copy of the
*Feasting Naturally* Newsletter . . . . . . . . . . . . . . . . . . **FREE**

_____ I am interested in Wholesale Distributorships . . . . **FREE**

_____ Please place me on the Priority Mailing
List for the *Feasting Naturally* Collection . . . . . . . . **FREE**

Postage and Handling (4 or fewer copies) . . . . . . . . **$.95**

TOTAL . . . . . . . . . . . _____

Name: _____

Address: _____

City: _____ State: _____ Zip: _____

Send check or money order to:

**Feasting....Naturally**
P.O. Box 968
Harrison, Arkansas 72601
501-741-7340

★ All Trade Orders (5 copies or more $4.80/copy) . . . . **40% Discount**

★ All **Prepaid Trade** orders . . . . . . . . . . . . . . . . . . . . . . . **FREIGHT FREE**

★ We accept telephone orders, S.T.O.P. orders, Mastercard and VISA.